MODERN MONTESSORI AT HOME

*A Creative Teaching Guide
for Parents of Children
Six through Nine Years of Age*

HEIDI ANNE SPIETZ

American Montessori Consulting
Rossmoor, California

i

ABOUT THE AUTHOR

Heidi Anne Spietz, author of "Montessori at Home" and "Modern Montessori at Home" holds a B.Sc. degree from REX University of N.Y., Albany and a diploma in Montessori training. In 1979 she was awarded, but declined because of other commitments, the prestigious CORO award. She holds general memberships in both the American Montessori Society and Association Montessori Internationale, Netherlands Chapter. She is well acquainted with how the Montessori method is used in the United States and in Europe, because she received her training from London, England. She has taught at private schools in the United States while concurrently managing her own successful tutoring business for the past five years.

Although the author and publisher has exhaustively researched all sources to ensure the accuracy and completeness of the information contained in this book, no responsibility is assumed for errors, inaccuracies, omissions or any other inconsistency herein. Any slights against people or organizations are unintentional.

Library of Congress Cataloging-in-Publication Data
Spietz, Heidi Anne
Modern Montessori at Home: a creative teaching guide for parents of children six through nine years of age / Heidi Anne Spietz
p. cm.
Bibliography: p.
Includes index.
ISBN 0-929487-02-8 : $9.95
1. Montessori method of education. 2. Home schooling-United States. I. Title.
LB775.M8S758 1989 89-14870
649'.124-dc20

This book is dedicated to my family members, Carl, Frances and Susan. I thank them for their love and encouragement. A special thanks goes to my mother, Frances, for her artistic input into the making of this book.

Thanks also to Dr. Edwin Brosbe, of California State Unviersity, Long Beach. He made the study of microbiology fascinating and challenging for his students. I think of him often when I present science lessons to my students and hope that I have inspired them in the way that he inspired his students.

I also owe much to Mr. Wellington and Mrs. Louise Blake of East Middle School. They made learning literature and grammar fascinating as well as meaningful.

A very special thanks to the people of the Happy One Hour Photo of Seal Beach, California for their superb job with the photography, and to the owners of Plaza Insta Print of Los Alamitos, California for the manufacturing of this book.

TABLE OF CONTENTS

Chapter 1
INTRODUCTION

Maria Montessori's philosophy has certainly stood the test of time. First introduced during the late 1800's, her method continues to be implemented in schools around the world. Acceptance of her method transcends differences in culture, language, or religion. For, her remarkable insight into the mission of the child is appreciated by all enlightened people who read her books.

Modern Montessori at Home, a sequel to **Montessori at Home,** is for both the elementary school teacher and parents of children six through nine years of age. This book builds on knowledge introduced in **Montessori at Home: A Complete Guide to Teaching Your Preschooler at Home Using the Montessori Method.** It is suggested that you obtain a copy of **Montessori at Home** so that your child will be able to derive the most from Montessori learning experiences.

Montessori at Home offers a complete beginning to phonics and reading for children three to five years of age. However, if your child, whatever his age may be, is experiencing difficulty with phonics, reading or spelling, use **Montessori at Home** to give him the groundwork he needs. Then, continue with the exercises in **Modern Montessori at Home.**

Likewise, if your child is not interested in geography or science, use the exercises in **Montessori at Home** to instill enthusiasm. Once his interest is sparked, then proceed with the geography and science lessons in **Modern Montessori at Home.**

If you are an elementary school teacher who wishes to use some of the Montessori methods in your classroom first read Chapters 1 and 2 thoroughly. A synopsis of the Montessori philosophy is presented in these two chapters along with some examples of how her method is applied in learning situations. Montessori's concept of a teacher and what a teacher's role should be is often in conflict with what is accepted in a public school environment. However, some public school districts are showing acceptance of Montessori's methods. So, possibly, in the not so distant future, we will see some changes in the curriculum that are reflective of this positive interest.

If you tutor children on a one to one basis, you have the unique opportunity of using all of the ideas in this book during your learning sessions. Children love creativity and will appreciate the chance to express themselves and actually experience in some cases what has been learned up until now from a textbook. By all means, encourage your students to become participants in the learning sessions.

If you travel to the student's house, bring in a chalkboard for the diagraming exercises mentioned on page 133. If the student is studying about rocks and minerals bring in some samples to show him and encourage him to look for some rocks on his own. When you present the geography lessons mentioned in this book, take a moment to draw a simple map, and then xerox a copy of it. See pages 110 and 111. If possible, obtain the stamps needed to present the Stamps of America exercise. Or, you may arrange for the parent and child to obtain some of the stamps so that you, the parent and child will be involved in this fun learning exercise.

I know that obtaining these learning aids is a bit time consuming, because I have actually taken the time to do this with my own students. However, the rewards are more than worth any inconvenience you may experience. The children become excited about the learning experience, and because their will is involved they truly benefit from it.

If you are a parent wishing to supplement your child's education at home, use this book as a tool for ideas on how you can offer your child additional learning exercises in phonics, reading, spelling, English grammar, composition, foreign languages, vocabulary building, nutrition, biology, geography, geology and history. Often, these subjects are presented in a vacuum, so your child can not see how one discipline actually relates to another. By using a little creative lesson planning, you can present lessons involving two disciplines during one learning session without your child actually realizing it. Your child will come away from the learning session with a sense of accomplishment, because he will have been an active rather than a passive participant. He will be encouraged to use some of his own initiative, rather than have a person dictate to him what he should study, and how much time should be spent studying it.

You may encounter a little resistance at first. Especially, if your child has been conditioned to react in a certain manner in a traditional school environment. He may feel that you are forcing him to do something that he has been conditioned to dislike. However, if you break the pattern by using some of the suggestions in this book, any initial obstinance will be overcome. Soon, he will discover that learning can be fun and challenging. Moreover, your child will appreciate this special time that the two of you spend together.

Keep in mind that in many public schools, there is 1 teacher for every 25 students at a given grade level. This is a terrific burden for the teacher as well as for the child. It is virtually impossible for the teacher to give each student all of the individualized attention that is needed. Some dedicated teachers make valiant efforts, but the burden is overwhelming and in time the result is stress burn out for the teacher.

Therefore, you have to take the initiative to make sure that your child gets the most from his formative learning years. This book will give you some ideas to start with, and by using a little brainstorming you will formulate other ideas as well!

Chapter II
THE MONTESSORI METHOD
FOR THE 1990's

The 1990's will present many challenges for the Montessori teacher. New innovations in technology will create some changes in the Montessori school environment. Computers are already commonplace in some Montessori schools in the United States. The emphasis on computer literacy for our children has crossed over from the public schools into the private educational domain, and some Montessori administrators in particular have shown a keen interest in integrating a computer learning program into the curriculum.

Changes in the Educational Environment

Some educational publishing firms now offer the classics like MacBeth, Black Beauty and the like on videocassettes as well as in book form to be used for school and home use. One publishing firm, Cambridge Press, has recently introduced the *Young Discovery Library*, which will undoubtedly revolutionize encyclopedias for children.

Changes in the learning environment, however, must only be made if they will help the child to function more effectively in today's society. Obviously, since computers have an integral function in our society the child needs to become computer literate. Thus, computer learning becomes a necessity.

Continued Need for the Montessori Method

To lose sight of Montessori's mission, however, would be a tragic mistake. We must not let technological advances interfere with the Montessori philosophy on which her teaching methods are based. Rather, we must consider the following very carefully when we instruct the child.

First, we must be certain that the child's physical, emotional and social needs are met. If the child is healthy, emotionally secure and enjoys interacting with other children he will feel more relaxed in a learning setting.

Typical Montessori Learning Environment

In a typical Montessori school the learning environment is carefully planned. There are designated areas for reading, science and so on. The rooms, furniture and learning materials are brightly colored so that the child will find the environment attractive. He is able to freely move about to select the materials that he will work with. Because the materials are neat and organized he is able to readily locate what is needed. He can then request that the teacher present the concept to him. If the concept was presented during the previous learning session he may request that the presentation be repeated. Such a request is not unusual. Often, a child may forget some of the steps involved in mastering a concept during the first presentation. Thus, this review serves to solidify the concept in his mind.

Importance of Presentation

The presentation is perhaps the most important function of the Montessori teacher. She must spend the necessary time to prepare the presentation. Often, the teacher will rehearse it, to make sure that all of the necessary steps are included. If during the rehearsal, she discovers that some steps have been omitted, she can easily rectify these errors before she makes the actual presentation to the child. All steps needed to master a concept should be presented in the appropriate order. This sequential order allows the child to see the logic of each step involved in the concept as a whole.

The Child's Journey

The child is on a journey which begins at birth. He enters the world as one who is dependent upon others for his survival and leaves this world as one who has made some impact on the environment around him.

As a society we must consider what educational experiences will benefit our children the most. Will we provide a boring, unstimulating learning environment for our children? Can we expect them to feel fulfilled and excited about learning if we bombard them with textbooks and multiple choice tests during their formative school years? How can we expect our children to make the discoveries and solve future global problems if they haven't had the opportunity to develop their creative intellectual capacities to the fullest.

Maria Montessori, I believe, had the answers to these and other significant questions concerning the education of our young. For she was wise enough to see that it is actually the child who is the 'teacher'. With the help of a guide the child learns what he needs to know as he progresses on his journey to becoming a self-actualized adult.

The Teacher as a Guide

The teacher guides the child during the learning session, but she does not impose her will on the child. She is enthusiastic and encouraging but never overbearing. Her patience is rewarded by the child's eagerness to master the concept or task.

When the child sees a task that he can comprehend and perform his will is attracted to it. The teacher can visibly see the expression of satisfaction written upon the child's face. The child is totally involved with the activity. He enthusiastically repeats the action over and over again, learning something new about himself and his environment each time he does. By uniting his body, mind, and will a sense of 'oneness' is felt.

Montessori Teacher of the 1990's

The Montessori teacher of the 1900's will need to use creative lesson planning to present the multitude of concepts that our children must be acquainted with. She must present lessons that will be both relevant to the child's future as well as satisfy his present needs. She must constantly search for innovative teaching ideas that will satisfy his curiosity yet allow him to ponder about world issues around him.

Children as Decision Makers of the Future

Our children will be the next generation of teachers, lawyers, doctors, architects, scientists, policy makers and so on. Moreover, as voters, they will be given the responsibility to make decisions on important issues. Therefore, we must provide the child with a prepared environment where he can develop his reasoning power to the fullest.

Because the Montessori philosophy can be easily applied in a home setting as well as in a school setting, it is imperative that we as teachers and parents see that our children learn in such an atmosphere. For if we give our children the proper tools in which to make intelligent choices, their decisions will benefit rather than destroy mankind.

Chapter III
THE ART OF PLANNING

Creating stimulating lessons can be an exciting experience for the parent or Montessori school teacher. Think of a dull lesson that you received as child. Now, think of an exciting one. Do you remember why it was exciting? You probably felt that the presenter was involved with the presentation. The presenter was excited about what he was communicating and you could feel that he was trying to reach each member of the class. To involve his students he used creative lesson planning.

Creative lesson planning requires careful consideration of multiple factors that are involved with the process of learning. These include defining the objective, considering the child's ability to appreciate the concept to be learned, allocating a sufficient amount of time for presentation and practice, preparing the lesson, and allowing for some flexibility during the learning session.

Once these factors have been considered the presenter can devote her time to giving the best presentation possible. She can spend time researching the topic to be discussed. She may even make a few field trips so that she can discuss the topic with experts. For example, if the presenter will be giving a presentation on rocks and minerals she may want to visit a shop specializing in rocks and minerals. She may talk to a geologist at a nearby college, or visit a museum exhibit of unique rocks and gems.

She may also visit her local library and borrow a videocassette on rock collecting or on other geological topics. She will then narrow this topic. Her objectives will be clearly defined, so that her presentation will be easily understood.

As you use the lesson plans included in this book, refer to this chapter from time to time to review creative lesson planning techniques. Each of the important elements in creative planning has been included for your convenience.

Defining the Objective

First, you need to define what you want your child to gain from the learning session. For example, if you are presenting the Classified Reading Exercise of a Plant you may want your child to be able to identify the different parts of the plant, state the functions of each part, and describe how these parts work together. Your child may give vague or incorrect answers during the initial learning session. However, his answers will become more thoughtful and accurate during subsequent learning sessions.

Never stress that you are giving your child a test. Rather, pose your questions in a natural way, so that your child feels uninhibited. For example, questions concerning the Classified Reading Exercises of a Plant would be posed during an informal discussion on gardening. Maria Montessori felt that children learn by doing. Thus, your child may benefit from "hands-on" experience involving gardening. The Classified Reading Cards Exercises of a Plant would also be more meaningful to him.

Considering the Child's Ability

Next, consider your child's ability. Children learn at different rates. For example, if your child is experiencing a little difficulty with the phonics exercises discussed in Chapter 4 in this book, you may want to consider obtaining a copy of **Montessori at Home. Montessori at Home: A Complete Guide to Teaching Your Preschooler at Home Using the Montessori Method** contains lesson plans to be used by parents of three to five year olds. A complete introduction to phonics is given in this book, and although **Montessori at Home** is designed to assist preschoolers, many six and seven year olds benefit from this phonetic review as well.

It is imperative that your child learn at his own pace. He should not feel pressured to master what he is not yet capable of mastering. Pushing a child to learn a concept that he cannot yet grasp leaves a child feeling frustrated and resentful. Be aware of your child's needs and allow him to express his desire to move forward. He will let you know when he is ready for the next step of learning.

Allotment of Time Must be Considered

Be aware of the time element involved in learning a given concept. For example, when introducing the Diagraming Exercises on page 133-138 allow sufficient time for chalkboard review. Children love to think up their own sentences and diagram them on the chalkboard. However, diagraming is quite time consuming and the child needs to feel relaxed to truly benefit from the exercise.

Present the exercises in a prepared environment. In such an environment, all the implements needed to properly present a concept are close at hand. When presenting the Stamps of America exercise you will need to draw or purchase a map of the United States and 50 different state stamps, one for each state of the union. However, a world globe and some selected issues of *National Geographic* are additional implements that you may consider using for the presentation of the exercise.

Flexible Lesson Planning

Flexibility is an essential component to productive learning sessions. Your child may have been so fascinated with a concept that you presented during a previous session that he may wish to continue working with it. This should not be discouraged. Take this time to review the concept that was presented during a previous session and allow extra time for your child to practice what he has learned.

Three Period Lesson

Montessori was inspired by the brilliant scientist, Seguin, and she was particularly impressed with Seguin's theory of the Three Period Lesson. The Three Period Lesson is successfully used in Montessori schools to assist three to five year olds in learning to recognize colors, shapes, numbers and the alphabet to name a few.

15

The Three Period Lesson can also be used to assist six to nine year olds in learning various concepts. The Three Period Lesson consists of "presenting" a child with a new concept, asking the child to "show you" that he understands what has been presented and ultimately determining if he can correctly "identify" and "pronounce" the name of the new concept that you have presented to him.

Let's use the Three Period Lesson to illustrate how you can help your child learn continent identification.

First, draw an outline of North America. Then, on a separate sheet of paper, draw an outline of South America. Do not label these outlines.

Period One – Place the outline of North America in front of your child. Next, state that this outline represents "North America". Then, place the outline of South America in front of your child and tell your child that this represents "South America". When you say "North America" or "South America" raise your voice slightly and emphasize these words a bit. Repeat Period One again before proceeding on to Period Two.

Period Two – Place the outlines of North America and South America in front of your child. Ask your child to show you the outline of South America. Then ask him to show you North America. Next, mix the outlines. Once again ask your child to show you the outline of North America. Then, ask him to show you the outline of South America.

16

Period Three – You will now want to determine if your child can clearly identify South
America and North America. Place the outline of
South America in front of him and ask him to tell
you the name of this continent. Your child should
respond by clearly saying the name. Repeat this
exercise with the outline of North America. Then,
introduce the other continents in the same
manner.

The Three Period Lesson can also be used to
help your child learn the names of plants, animals,
musical instruments and so on. It is essential
though that the Three Period Lesson be presented
in a relaxed setting. Never rush through the Three
Period Lesson. Allow enough time for Period One
and Period Two. In some cases you may have to
repeat Period One or Period Two before proceeding
on to Period Three. Keep in mind that your child
will understand more fully if he is encouraged to
absorb the knowledge at his own rate.

The Role of the Presenter

As a presenter you must be armed with the
knowledge you need to make a good presentation.
Anticipate the questions your child may ask and
then jot them down. If you are not sure of the
answers, do a little research at the library. While at
the library, you may also want to browse through
the children's section to see if you can find any

interesting books on the subject you will be presenting.

Your role is to present the lesson. A Montessori teacher first presents a concept to the child and once she is satisfied that the child understands the principles involved she removes herself and allows the child to work with the concept on his own. She is a quiet observer; however, she is there to assist if the child has a question about the activity he is engaged in.

The Montessori teacher is encouraging and calm. The child views her as a companion and a helper. He trusts her, because he feels that she has a genuine love and respect for him.

The presenter simply presents the concepts. However, it is the child, while working with the concepts, who makes the discoveries and spontaneous explosions that are associated with learning. To see a child's face reflect the joy from gaining new insight, however, is the ultimate reward for any Montessori teacher or parent.

Chapter 4
CREATIVE LESSON PLANNING FOR
FIRST AND SECOND GRADERS

The first or second grader of today is quite different from the typical six or seven year old of 20 years ago. The children of the 1980's have been exposed to a fast paced, highly automated society. For example, many libraries, bookstores, banks and other businesses have their records kept on computers. The child's mother may use an automated telling machine to do her banking, pay for her groceries and gasoline.

Some children, as young as three years of age, have been exposed to the home computer. As tots, they were intrigued by the flurry of figures and letters dancing across the screen. They watched as their parents did the banking, bookkeeping or even in some households, the family shopping on this curious little machine.

Their older siblings may have used the home computer to complete homework assignments. The vast array of cartridges and tapes one can buy for these home computers is simply mind boggling. Many parents have felt that the home computer is a tool that the family just can't do without.

Another educational tool, the VCR, is as commonplace in the home as the FAX machine will some day become. A diverse selection of educational cassettes is easily accessible to the VCR consumer. Undoubtedly, many children have been exposed to phonics, spelling and other basic learning skills via the family's VCR.

It's no wonder then that the typical first or second grade class at a private or public schools is vastly different from their counterparts of two or three decades ago. Hence, it is the job of parents and teachers to realize this when we plan learning activities for them. We must provide a balanced learning environment that reflects what modern technology has to offer while still incorporating Montessori's philosophy of allowing the child to make his own discoveries.

Integrating More than One Subject into a Lesson

While you are busy preparing the environment, keep in mind how essential it is that your child sees the relationship of one discipline to another, i.e. geography to science, comparative literature to history and even phonics to spelling. A subject should never be taught in a vacuum. If each subject is presented separately, your child will fail to see the whole picture. A piece meal educational learning experience is a frustrating one for your child and an unrewarding one for the parent or teacher.

Fun Filled Phonics and Reading Exercises for the First and Second Grader

Phonics can be presented in such a way that the child becomes bored and disinterested in participating in further exercises. In such a negative setting, the child is required to write long lists of words, memorize rules that he can't apply or doesn't understand and relate what he has learned to the correct pronunciation of words. It is no wonder that such an experience leaves the child feeling discouraged.

Conversely, if phonics is presented in a prepared environment, complete with exciting learning tools and by a relaxed, encouraging presenter, i.e. the parent or teacher, the child will be eager to particpate. The following exercises are the "tools" that are designed to give your child hours of enjoyment and learning. Remember, to present the exercises in a clear, concise way. Allow plenty of time for your child to complete each exercise and encourage him with praise for every small success.

wh	br	gr	ph
what	brim	grip	phone
when	bring	gripe	photo
wheat	braid	grape	phase
where	bride	grin	
whale	brave		
why			

Phonogram Exercise

Phonograms like the ones pictured on page 22 can be provided in a colorful way so that your child appreciates the following activities even more. See pages 42-46 for a complete chart of the phonograms that you will need to use for the following exercises.

First, you will need to purchase index or flash cards measuring 3" x 9" or 3" x 5" in a vast array of colors. As an alternative, you may wish to purchase a multi-color packet of construction paper. If you use construction paper to make the cards, trim the cards so that they measure either 3" x 9" or 3" x 5".

You may want to purchase sheets of construction paper or cards in various shades of colors, i.e. light orange, red orange, light green, blue-green and so on. Each color will represent a different category of the decoding. For example, you may want to use light green cards for all words containing the "wh" phonogram. Then, write words like "wheat" "what" "where" "why" and "when" on the light green cards. Once you have exhausted "wh" words gather the cards together and place them in a single pile. Next, select a different color to introduce the "ph" phonogram. Write the "ph" words on cards and place them together in a second pile. Continue until you have several phonogram piles.

You will want to present a few cards at a time, and be sure to use the Three Period Lesson to determine if your child is decoding and pronouncing the words correctly. If you haven't read **Montessori at Home** and aren't familiar with Montessori's Three Period Lesson, then you will want to reread page 16 of this book before proceeding with the exercise.

Your child will love this color coded exercise even more when you announce that you and he are about to play Phonogram Bingo. To prepare for this game you will need to make up about 15 game cards. The cards should measure about 9" x 12". You can make the cards out of construction paper, or as an alternative, use lightweight posterboard. I have found that the posterboard works best. Both items should be available at your neighborhood stationery store or art supply store. Purchase a few extra sheets of construction paper or lightweight posterboard so that you can make plenty of markers. These markers should be the diameter of a quarter. Choose any color that you like. Perhaps you will want to select your child's favorite color. You will need six markers per game card. Since only you and your child will initially play this game, a total of twelve markers will be needed.

Select two piles of phonogram cards, i.e., "wh" and "ph". Mix the two piles together and after you have sufficiently shuffled the cards, make one new pile, Then, from the top of the pile, select three phonogram cards and print one word in the upper left half of the game card, print the second word in the upper middle half of the game card and print the third word in the upper right half of the game card. See page 25. If you use the "wh" and "ph" phonograms you may have a combination of word like wheat, photo and phone for the top row. From the phonogram pile, select three more cards and print the fourth word in the lower left half, print the fifth word in the middle lower half and print the sixth word in the lower right half area of the game card. You may want to draw one line horizontally and two lines vertically to separate the words printed on top from the words printed on the bottom of the card. Either way, continue selecting phonogram cards, three at a time, and completing the game cards until you have finished 15 or more.

Phonogram Bingo Game

Now you and your child are set to have some fun! Invite your child to select a game card. You, in turn will also select one. Next, go through the phonogram cards and remove the cards that have the identical words that are on your child's game board. Glance at your own game board. Let's suppose that on the top half of your game card the words wheat, photo, and phone appear, and that on the bottom half the words where, while, and whale appear. You will then proceed to remove the wheat, where, while, whale, photo, and phone phonogram cards. You should have removed a total of 12 phonogram cards from the pile, six of which are identical to your child's game card and six of which are identical to your game card.

Now, shuffle the 12 phonogram cards and stack them in one pile. Give your child six markers and take six for yourself. Explain to your child that he should select the top phonogram card from the pile of 12 and tell you what it says. He then must look carefully at his game card to see if he can find the word on either the top half or bottom half. If he can, tell him to put a marker over the word. Now, you must look carefully at your game card. You may want to hesitate a bit, and encourage your child to help you look. He will enjoy doing so, and this will give him extra practice in reading and phonics. If you see the word on your game card you must place a marker over it. Now, it is your turn to take the next card from the top. You will read it and then both of you will look to see on which game card the word appears. The first person who has three markers across, either top row or bottom row wins the game!

During other learning sessions together, you and your child can play this fun bingo game with phonics prefix cards. Once again you will use color coded index cards. You will want to include words beginning with prefixes like "en" in enjoy, "un" unhappy, "re" in return, "al" in always and "be" in besides to name a few. You may decide to use light blue index cards for words containing the "en" prefix, dark blue for words beginning with the "un" prefix and so on. You and your child can decide just how colorful you want the exercise to be. You may prefer to use just one shade of each color or many shades of each color.

Obviously, a phonics discussion wouldn't be complete without mentioning the importance of studying suffixes. For some reason suffixes trouble some children. The suffix "ed" in particular creates problems for some children when they read aloud. A child may read the following sentence in this manner. *The mother cook-ed some stew.* The word cooked is pronounced as though it contained two syllables instead of one. Therefore, in order to provide your child with a clear understanding of how "ed" words are pronounced, it is often useful to list these words using two different color coded piles of index cards. Make this exercise colorful by selecting two different vibrant colors like orange and turquoise.

Think of as many words as possible that end with the suffix "ed" and consist of only one syllable. At this point, it is not advisable to introduce words that required dropping the "e" as in the word pine, i.e. pine + ed = pined. Nor should you include words which require adding an ending consonant, i.e. pin + ned = pinned. You should only include words like mailed, sailed, failed, wailed, turned, churned, billed, willed, drilled, milled, filled, fished, wished, dished, and so on. See page 46.

Now take the turquoise colored cards that you set aside, and print each of the one syllable "ed" ending words on these cards, one word per card. Your child may want to help you print the words on these cards, and you should encourage him to do so. Remind him to print neatly, so that he will be able to easily read what he has printed.

Once you are finished printing the words on the turquoise colored cards, stack them together in a pile, and prepare to print two syllable "ed" words on the orange cards. You may wish to include words like pounded, sounded, rounded, fainted, painted, mended, bended, baited, waited, stated, faded, rated, and tested. See page 46 for a list of possible two syllable words that you may want to present.

You can make another fun bingo game using these cards by mixing the orange, two syllable "ed" words with the turquoise, one syllable "ed" words into one pile and then by following the rest of the directions for the Phonogram Bingo game. Or, you can invite your child to put words in alphabetical order. First, the child would alphabetize the one syllable "ed" words and later he would alphabetize the two syllable "ed" words. Finally, you may want to shuffle some of the orange two syllable "ed" words with some of the turquoise one syllable "ed" words and invite him to alphabetize all of them.

You will want to introduce "ing" endings using the preceding exercises, with one exception. Choose two different vibrant colors like yellow and kelly green for the one and two syllable "ing" words. It is important not to include words that require adding an ending consonant to the root, i.e., skip + ped = skipped. Nor should you include words that require dropping the "e" as in the word savᵉ + ed = saved. See page 47 for examples of one and two syllable words ending in "ing".

The following rules and examples must not be memorized by your child. Rather, you should encourage your child to analyze the words and recognize certain similarities and differences in how the suffixes are added. For example, he sees that words like tag, bag, fit, mop and rub all end in one consonant and have the short vowel sound. He soon recognizes that he must double the final consonant before adding "ing" or "ed". Conversely, when he analyzes words like make, file and rope he becomes aware of how he must drop the "e" before adding "ing" or "ed". Hopefully, he remembers the two vowel rule that he learned in kindergarten, i.e. when there are two vowels in a one syllable word, we say the first vowel with its long sound, while the second vowel is silent. The child remembers that a monosyllable word like *beat* is pronounced with its long "e" vowel sound, while the "a" is silent. Therefore, he does not say "be""at".

RULE 1:   When a word ends with one consonant and the vowel sound is short, we must double the consonant before adding "ed" or "ing".

EXAMPLE: ROOT WORD ED SUFFIX ING SUFFIX
                HOP   HOPPED   HOPPING

RULE 2:   When a word ends with one consonant and the vowel sound is short, we must double the consonant before adding "er".

EXAMPLE: ROOT WORD EST SUFFIX ER SUFFIX
                FAT   FATTEST   FATTER

RULE 3:   When a monosyllable word has two vowels we say the first vowel with its long sound while the second vowel is silent. Thus, if this word ends in silent "e", we must drop the "e" before adding "ed" or "ing".

EXAMPLE: ROOT WORD ED SUFFIX ING SUFFIX
                HIKE   HIKED   HIKING

RULE 4:   If a word ends in silent "e", we must drop the "e" when adding "er" or "est".

EXAMPLE: ROOT WORD ER SUFFIX ING SUFFIX
                NICE   NICER   NICEST

To make this next exercise challenging for your child you will want to make up root cards and suffix cards like the ones pictured on page 32. Once again, index cards work well for this exercise; however, if you prefer to use construction paper or lightweight posterboard, cut the cards so they measure 3" x 5". You may want to color code this exercise using blue index cards for the root words, pink index cards for "ed" suffixes, white index cards for "ing" suffixes, and so on. On a separate colored card make one diagonal line. You will see the purpose for doing so in a moment. Look at page 32 for an illustration of how this exercise is done.

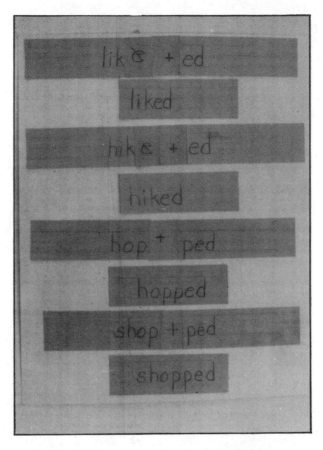

Root and Suffix Endings Exercise

First, using blue index cards, write the root words, one on each card. Page 47 has a chart of some words that you may wish to include.

Using pink index cards, print the "ed" suffixes. Look carefully at the root words that you have chosen to include in your presentation.

If you have included words like hop, mop, pat and so on, you will need to make a "ped" card so that when your child combined the root card **hop** with the "ped" card he will have formed a new word, **hopped**. By printing the consonant plus "ed" your child sees that the ending consonant in these short vowel words must be doubled. He then proceeds to combine the root card **mop** with the suffix "ped" (mop + ped) to form **mopped**. Moreover, if you have chosen to include the root word **mob** you must make a "bed" suffix card so that your child can form mob + bed = **mobbed**.

Look at the illustration for adding suffixes to words with the silent "e". Notice with the word "like" that a card with a line is placed over the "e" to cross it out, i.e. likℓ. Your child first places the card with the − on it over the "e" and then proceeds to place the "ed" or "ing" card on top. This reminds the child that he must remove the "e" before adding the "ed" or "ing" suffix when he prints the word.

Sailing through Spelling

Spelling need not be a tedious exercise that your child learns to dread. Rather, learning to spell can be one of the most enjoyable activities that your child experiences. The key, once again, is preparing the appropriate environment. If your child sees that learning how to spell is both fun and relevant, then he will be an enthusiastic participant.

By using a little creative planning, you can incorporate two learning adventures into one lesson. Most children love to learn more about the beach, the mountains, rural living, i.e., life on a farm, life in a desert, and the like. Therefore, you can create a spelling list of words that deal with the flora and fauna of a beach environment, or you may want to use one of the other preceding examples. As a teacher and tutor, I have always found that children love learning more about the beach. Obviously, because most of the children I teach live near the beach, they have spent many enjoyable times there. Consequently, the children are receptive to a spelling lesson covering this topic.

The following one syllable words are good for beginning spellers: whale, shark, beach, sand, shell, rock, waves, crab, and fish. Later, you may want to include two syllable words like ocean, water and seaweed.

You probably have a set of encyclopedias at home; if not, you will need to borrow a set from a friend or relative for this spelling exercise. If pos-

34

sible, borrow a set that is designed for the beginning student. You will find that the set of encyclopedias for beginners contains many colorful pictures; moreover, the print is larger and easier for the young child to read and comprehend.

Read about whales, sharks and any other oceanographic topics that relate to the other words in the spelling list. If you do not have a set encyclopedias, but you do subscribe to *National Geographic,* you may find an interesting article relating to the ocean and/or beach. Moreover, you will undoubtedly see some beautiful pictures accompanying the article that your child will enjoy.

Whether you use the encyclopedias or an article from *National Geographic,* you will want to make notes as you read. In particular, note the differences and similarities in the beach environments around the world, both flora and fauna. Make notes that compare, for example, the beaches in the United States with the beaches in South America. Obviously, if you are obtaining your information from *National Geographic* you will make notes about the beach that is described in the article. Jot down anything that you think might interest your child, i.e. the difference between low tide and high tide, water pollution, and so on. Be sure to research the subject thoroughly, because children are known to be inquisitive, and they are delighted when we can satisfy their curiosity.

Next, using index cards, invite your child to neatly print his spelling words, one per card, by

35

referring to the word list that you have given to him. Encourage him to notice the different phonetic patterns like "wh" in <u>wh</u>ales, "cr" in <u>cr</u>ab and so on. Allow ample time for him to complete this exercise. Do not pressure him to finish quickly. Once he is finished, then you and he are set for an exciting adventure.

With the index cards handy, show your child one of the magazine pictures which clearly illustrates one of his spelling words. If you used encyclopedias, then you probably have multiple pictures which you will use for your presentation of the spelling words. As an example, let's suppose that you are showing your child a picture of a whale. Ask your child to locate the index card, which for this discussion will be referred to as "the label" with the word <u>whale</u> printed on it. Then, invite him to put this label underneath the picture of the whale. Hopefully, you will have studied a little about the different kinds of whales, i.e. gray whale, blue whale, true's bead whale and the southern-bottlenosed whale to name a few, so that you and your child can have an enlightening discussion on the subject of whales. Your child will enjoy looking through the magazines or encyclopedias which illustrate his spelling words. It will be challenging for him to find the appropriate labels for these pictures. Moreover, your child will discover the wonderful world of encyclopedias. He will see pictures that relate to other topics and this will give the two of you a chance to have discussions about other educational topics. If your child is using an encyclopedia for beginners, by all means show him how to use it. This is one tool that he will want to use again in the near future.

If at all possible, take your child on a field trip to the beach. It may be true that a picture is worth a thousand words, but there is no substitute for the real thing. There is nothing like the feeling of a gentle breeze blowing the hair away from your face, or the scent of salt water permeating the air to make one appreciate the beach environment. It is there, at the beach, that you and your child can review what was discussed at home. Put this time to good use. If possible, go on a "whale watching" excursion. Other activities you may want to include are looking for seashells and discussing where they came from, reviewing topics like low tide, high tide, and so on.

The fun can continue at home with an exercise I call the Alphabet Spelling Game. The Movable Alphabet can be easily constructed; the only implements needed are a packet of index cards and a pencil. Print each of the letters of the alphabet, one on each card, from A to Z. Make five sets of the alphabet because many words use more than one letter. For example, the word s<u>e</u>aw<u>ee</u>d requires three e's; two l's are required to spell the words she<u>ll</u>, and so on.

First with the spelling list handy, select three words from the spelling list. For example, if you select fish, crab and shell, you will need to remove the following letters from the Movable Alphabet Sets, f, i, s, h, c, r, a, b, s, h, e, l, l.

Next, shuffle the letters that you removed and then spread them out so they can be easily read. Then invite your child to participate in the game. Locate the letters needed to spell s-h-e-l-l. Show your child how you retrieve s, h, e, l, l and then neatly line up the letters so that the word can be easily read. Now, you and your child can read the word together.

Next, invite your child to locate the letters needed to spell the word f-i-s-h. After he has retrieved the letters and has neatly lined them up, encourage him to read what he has spelled. Finally, invite him to spell the word "crab" in the same manner.

Continue the spelling game, by using three more words from the spelling list. To add a challenging dimension to this activity, you may want to ask your child to identify phonetic patterns, i.e. "cr" in crab, "sh" in shell, and in fish as he has previously done. Be sure to praise him for his accomplishments and allow him to see how delighted you are with his progress.

The preceding exercises can be successfully used to incorporate other disciplines as well. You can create a farm animal spelling list which would perhaps include words like cow, pig, horse, barn and farm. You may want to review the short "i" in pig, phonetic pattern of "ar" in barn and farm and "or" in horse if these words are included in your list. Use a set of encyclopedias or magazines about rural living to do your research. If you live near a farm, you may want to consider visiting one. Your child will love seeing these animals in their natural habitat.

The farm animal spelling list may also be easily incorporated into games like the Movable Alphabet Game. Just follow the directions for playing the geography spelling game and substitute the list of beach spelling words for farm animals words.

Hopefully, thus far, your child has enjoyed your learning sessions together. He has considered these sessions to be challenging and stimulating, rather than boring and tedious. You have given him the opportunity to discover first hand the relationship of reading to phonics and spelling to vocabulary. He sees that by changing the suffix or prefix of a root word, he changes its meaning. For example, he learns that the meaning of taste__less__ is very different from the meaning of taste__ful__.

Because you have given him the tools to make these discoveries he has gained more confidence in his ability to read. At this time, you should find that your child is quite receptive to acquiring more knowledge in this area, and he will appreciate the opportunity to refine his skills by practicing the following modern Montessori language exercises.

I have always stressed phonics while tutoring on a one to one basis or while teaching in a classroom setting. A child who reads phonetically can decode the word quickly and comprehend its meaning in context with other words in a sentence with less difficulty.

Encourage your child to practice these exercises. Be patient if he makes errors. If he feels that you are relaxed and that he is not pressured to finish his work at a specified time he will continue to be an active participant.

Blue-Series Phonogram Classification Cards

You can easily make the **Blue Series Phonogram Classification Cards** by using packets of 3" x 5" white index cards and crayons in eight different shades of blue. By purchasing a box of 64 crayons you should find most, if not all of the shades of blue that you need.

EXAMPLE: Print the following phonograms, one phonogram per index card, using a BLUE CRAYON

sh le or th wh ph ing dge tion cr dr ea oo

Refer to the following chart for color coding the remaining phonograms:

COLOR	PHONOGRAMS
(Crayon-Color)	
BLUE-GREEN	ie, i – e as in (nice) igh as in (high) -y as in (try)
LIGHT BLUE	ai as in (paid), ay, ei as in (rein), a - e as in (crane)
VIOLET BLUE	c as in (cent, city) g as in (general, giraffe)
MED. BLUE	oa as in (boat) ow as in (row), oe as in (toe)
NAVY BLUE	k as in (know, knot), w as in (wrong, write)
ROYAL BLUE	ir as in (bird, girl), ce as in (verse), ur as in (nurse)
BLUE-GRAY	ie as in (cookie), ee as in (meet), ea as in (meat), -y as in (penny)

40

Once you have finished, place the phonogram index cards in a pile, and explain to your child that these cards serve as color coded labels for this exercise. Further explain to him that they will be referred to as "labels" for the next exercise.

Next, have your child locate the phonogram cards that were used for the PHONOGRAM BINGO GAME. Explain to your child that he needs to place the appropriate phonogram cards under the corresponding label. For example, under the "oo" label he should place phonogram cards that have "oo" words printed on them like b<u>oo</u>k, l<u>oo</u>k, and c<u>oo</u>k.

Encourage your child to work with only two or three labels at first. Later, he may want to work with five or six. Eventually, once he is proficient, he will want to work with all of the labels.

This exercise gives your child further practice in decoding words. He sees that some words like church contain two phonogram "ch" and "ur". Therefore, he discovers that this word can be placed under the "ur" label or the "ch" label.

CHART 1
PHONOGRAMS

SC	SK	SM
SCAT	SKATE	SMOKE
SCAMPER	SKILL	SMILE
SCUFF	SKY	SMOOTH
SCANT	SKIT	SMELL

GR	SP	TW
GRIN	SPELL	TWIST
GREAT	SPIN	TWIN
GREET	SPECK	TWELVE
GRAY	SPAN	TWINE
GRASS	SPINE	TWILIGHT
GROVE	SPOIL	TWENTY
GRILL	SPOON	TWELVE
GREEN	CLASP	TWIG
GRIP	SPILL	TWEED

DGE	LL	TCH
BADGE	BALL	WITCH
FUDGE	CALL	MATCH
JUDGE	MALL	PATCH
BUDGE	STALL	MOUTH
PLEDGE	FALL	HATCH
EDGE	SHELL	LATCH
HEDGE	SPELL	CATCH

OUGHT	AUGHT	ILD
BROUGHT	CAUGHT	CHILD
FOUGHT	TAUGHT	MILD
SOUGHT	DAUGHTER	WILD
BOUGHT		

PHONOGRAMS

WR	PR	DR
WRINKLE	PRAY	DRUM
WRIST	PRIDE	DRIVE
WROUGHT	PROD	DROVE
WRAP	PRY	DRILL
WRING	PRIZE	DRINK
WRITE	PRUNE	DRAPE
WROTE	PRAISE	DREAM
WRONG	PRESS	DROP
WREATH	PRONE	DRIP
WRECK	PROP	DRIFT
WREN	PROBE	DRY

CL	FL	BL
CLAP	FLY	BLUE
CLIP	FLEW	BLOOM
CLIMB	FLAIR	BLAZE
CLOT	FLOWER	BLIGHT
CLUE	FLAKE	BLAST
CLEAN	FLOAT	BLAIR
CLEAR	FLEET	BLACK
CLOSE	FLAP	BLAME

FR	ST	GL
FROG	STOP	GLUE
FROZEN	STEEL	GLOB
FREEZE	STEM	GLOVE
FRILL	STOOD	GLIDE
FRAN	STRIVE	GLOAT
FRUIT	STALL	GLAD

PHONOGRAMS

TH	CR	CH
THIMBLE	CROSS	CHURCH
THING	CREST	CHAIN
TEETH	CRIB	CHILL
THIS	CROW	CHOOSE
THANK	CREW	CHECKERS
PATH	CRAB	CHAIR
THIN	CRANE	CHINESE
HATH	CREAM	CHALK
THEME	CRY	CHERRY
THUD	CRUST	BENCH
THINE	CRAWL	CHEEK
THUMB	CRADLE	CHEESE
THORN	CRACK	WHICH

SH	BR	WH
SHELL	BRUSH	WHISTLE
WASH	BRIGHT	WHICH
MESH	BRING	WHALE
FISH	BROUGHT	WHERE
SHINE	BROKE	WHEN
SHOES	BRICK	WHY
SHOVEL	BRUISE	WHISKERS
SHIRT	BRITTLE	WHEEL
BUSH	BRIDGE	WHINE
RUSH	BRIDE	WHIM

STR	SCR	OR
STRING	SCRAM	TAILOR
STRUNG	SCRUB	ELEVATOR
STRAW	SCREAM	DOCTOR

PHONOGRAMS

OO	OO	OY
MOON	BOOK	BOY
NOON	COOK	TOY
SOON	LOOK	JOY
BOOM	TOOK	OYSTER
LOOM	HOOK	
TOOTH	FOOT	
HOOT	WOOD	
ROOF	GOOD	

OR	OI
LORD	CHOICE
CHORD	MOIST
SWORD	COIN
TORN	JOIN
FORM	OIL

ING	ANG	INK
SPRING	BANG	BLINK
RING	SANG	SINK
BRING	RANG	RINK
	FANG	THINK
	SPRANG	

ANK	AY	ILD
BANK	PLAY	CHILD
SPANK	DAY	MILD
PLANK	PRAY	WILD
RANK	SAY	
	FAY	
	MAY	

PHONOGRAMS

IND	EW	LE
KIND	STEW	LITTLE
RIND	FLEW	GENTLE
BIND	BLEW	RUSTLE
FIND	CREW	MUSCLE
MIND	KNEW	BUSTLE
HIND	NEW	PUDDLE

EAR	EAR	STR
EARTH	TEAR	STRUNG
LEARN	BEAR	STRUNG
SEARCH	PEAR	STROKE

THR	SPL	SQU
THREE	SPLASH	SQUEAK
THRIVE	SPLINT	SQUASH
THREW	SPLIT	SQUIRM

CHART II
(ONE SYLLABLE WORDS) ROOT = ED

MAILED	TURNED	PRAYED
FAILED	BURNED	STAGED
BAILED	LEARNED	JOINED
SAILED	STAYED	DRILLED
HAILED	PLAYED	BILLED
FLOWED	STRAYED	FILLED

CHART III
(TWO SYLLABLE WORD) ROOT + ED

POUNDED	MENDED
SOUNDED	RENTED
ROUNDED	RATED
PAINTED	TESTED

46

CHART IV
(ONE SYLLABLE WORDS) ROOT + ING

MAILING	TURNING	PRAYING
FAILING	BURNING	STAGING
BAILING	LEARNING	JOINING
HAILING	STAYING	DRILLING
FLOWING	PLAYING	BILLING
POUNDING	FAINTING	STATING
SOUNDING	BENDING	FADING
ROUNDING	MENDING	RATING
PAINTING	RENTING	TESTING

CHART V
ROOT + DOUBLE CONSONANT + ING

ROB	ROBBING
MOP	MOPPING
LET	LETTING
KNIT	KNITTING
WRAP	WRAPPING

CHART VI
ROOT + DOUBLE CONSONANT + ED

STOP	STOPPED
MOP	MOPPED
WRAP	WRAPPED
SHOP	SHOPPED

CHART VII
ROOT – "E" + ING

LIKE	LIKING
MAKE	MAKING
WRITE	WRITING

47

CHART VIII
ROOT – "E" + ED

LIKE	LIKED
BAKE	BAKED
PHONE	PHONED

EXERCISES IN GRAMMAR

Maria Montessori used color coding to make grammar an enjoyable, meaningful experience for the young child. To introduce the parts of speech, specific colors were designed for nouns, verbs, adjectives, and the like. The following color coding is still used in Montessori schools today.

PARTS OF SPEECH	COLOR
Article	Gray
Noun	Black
Pronoun	Light Pink
Adjective	Blue
Verb	Red
Adverb	Orange
Conjunction	Purple/Mauve
Preposition	Green
Interjection	Yellow

Construction paper works well for this exercise, so purchase an inexpensive multi-color packet to make the parts of speech and phrase cards. Each card should measure about 3" x 5", so you will be able to make multiple cards from one sheet of construction paper.

Gray cards are used for the articles *a, an* and *the*. On the black noun cards print examples of *people, places* and *things,* i.e. Sam, Julie, house, school, shell, crab, girl and car. On the light pink pronoun cards print *he, she, they, I, we, it* and *you*. Adjectives like *pretty, funny, tall, short, happy* and *yellow* should be printed on blue cards. Include words like *jump, hop, stand, run,* and *sit* on red cards. On the orange adverb cards you will want to include words like *quietly, lightly, rarely, here, always.* Conjunctions like *and, or, nor, but* and *for* should be printed on purple or mauve colored cards. Prepositions like *in, out, on, up, over, around, under* and the like are printed on green cards. Finally, the interjections like *Oh!, Ah!* and *Ow!* are printed on yellow cards.

Start with the noun cards. Perhaps you can think of things around the house that you may want to include on these cards, i.e. chair, book, television, lamp, sweater, and so on. Explain to your child that nouns name people, places and things. Have him select one of the noun cards, read it and point to the object. For example, if he selects a card with the word "chair" on it, then he must point to the chair. Continue in this manner until he has selected at least five cards. Next, introduce the adjective. Explain to your child that an adjective describes people, places or things. Pick up a sweater and ask your child to tell you what color it is. Explain that the color is the adjective describing the sweater. It is advisable to make at least 10 adjective cards so that your child has plenty of practice identifying this part of speech. Your child may

49

confuse adjectives with adverbs, so it is important that he spends at least two learning sessions working with adjectives.

Next, explain to your child that instead of constantly referring to a person by his or her name, we use the pronouns "he" or "she" in place of the proper name. If you have a pet then you can use him as an example. Explain to your child that instead of referring to the pet Blacky as Blacky all of the time we say him or he. He is hungry. Give the food to him.

You can continue in the same manner explaining how the other parts of speech relate to your child's life. You should only introduce one new part of speech at a time, and be sure to review the parts of speech that were previously presented to your child from time to time. He will get new insight each time he reviews the parts of speech. The review time gives him the chance to see how the different parts of speech link together and form a meaningful sentence.

Grammar Trays

For this exercise you will need a small tray, color coded grammar cards, labels for each part of speech, i.e. a label which says ARTICLE, a label which says ADJECTIVE, a label which says NOUN, and phrase cards.

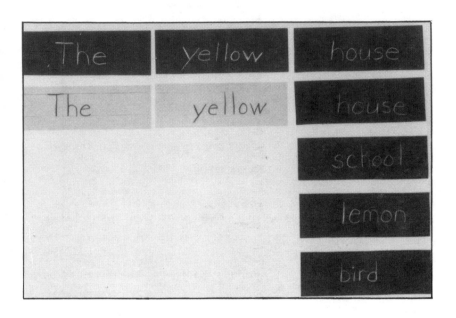

Noun Parsing Tray Exercise

Look at the picture of the Noun Tray on page 51. Notice how the phrase is dissected, according to the parts of speech involved.

THE YELLOW HOUSE
(Phrase Card - written on a black card)
BLACK = NOUN

ARTICLE	ADJECTIVE	NOUN
THE (Written on Gray Card)	**YELLOW** (Written on Blue Card)	**HOUSE** (Written on Black Card)

First, print a phrase on a long strip of black construction paper. You may also use lightweight posterboard. You may want to use the phrase <u>The Yellow House</u> for your first example, or you may want to select a different one on your own. Your phrase should consist of one article, one adjective and one noun. After you have printed the phrase on the black strip of construction paper, print the corresponding words which make up the phrase on color coded cards. For example, if you use the phrase, <u>The Yellow House,</u> you will need one gray card for the word "The", one blue card for the word "yellow" and one black card for the word "house".

You will need to make up four additional noun cards so that your child can fully appreciate the significance of the "noun". By changing the noun he sees that the meaning of the sentence is quite different.

EXAMPLE: THE YELLOW <u>**BIRD**</u>
        "   "   <u>**LEMON**</u>
        "   "   <u>**CAR**</u>

Notice in the preceding examples that only the noun has changed. Later, you will want to introduce a different phrase and four additional nouns that can be substituted.

EXAMPLE: THE YELLOW <u>**SHOES**</u>
        "   "   <u>**CARD**</u>
        "   "   <u>**SCHOOL**</u>
        "   "   <u>**DOG**</u>

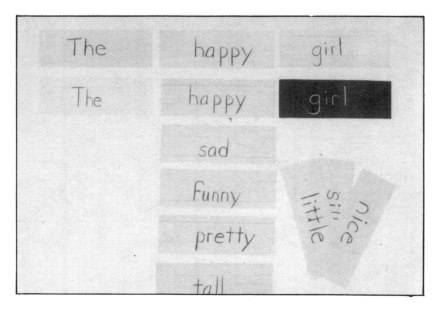

The Adjective Parsing Tray Exercise

Once again you will need to place a phrase in the upper part of the tray. See page 53 for a picture of this exercise.

THE ADJECTIVE TRAY

EXAMPLE: THE HAPPY GIRL
(Phrase Card - Written on a Blue Card)
BLUE = ADJECTIVE

ARTICLE	ADJECTIVE	NOUN
THE	**HAPPY**	**GIRL**
(Written on Gray Card	(Written on Blue Card	(Written on Black Card)

As you can see, the emphasis is now placed upon the adjective. The phrase is written on a blue strip of construction paper. The noun does not change. Rather, the child manipulates the adjective cards to change the meaning of the phrase.

For the phrase above, print THE HAPPY GIRL on a blue strip of construction paper. The article "The" is printed on a gray colored card, the adjective "happy" is printed on a blue colored card and the noun "girl" is printed on a black card. Make up four additional adjectives, i.e. sad, funny, pretty and tall.

EXAMPLE: THE HAPPY GIRL
"   SAD   "
"   FUNNY   "
"   PRETTY   "
"   TALL   "

54

This exercise may be continued with other parts of speech, i.e. verbs, adverbs, prepositions and the like. However, you will have to make new phrases, and keep in mind that the color of the phrase should be consistent with the color coding given on page 48. Impress upon your child that the color black per se does not represent a noun. Rather, the color coding is used to help distinguish the different parts of speech and make the exercise more meaningful to him.

Now that your child is becoming aware of how sentences are complete thoughts made up of verbs, nouns and possibly adjectives, adverbs and the like you will want to introduce another Montessori exercise. Once again you will notice that I have combined two disciplines during one learning session, i.e. grammar and social studies.

For this project, you will need to borrow a book on Indians that is written on the first or second grade level. You may want to borrow a book that provides a general overview of all American Indians or one that includes information about a specific tribe, i.e. Chippewa, Apache, Chinook, Sioux, and so on. You may want to borrow several books on the subjects and let your child select the one that he would enjoy reading.

Next, using construction paper make the following symbols. (Your child will be printing sentences on paper, and he will use these symbols to illustrate the parts of speech used in the sentences.)

The following coloring code is still used in Montessori Schools today.

ARTICLE	SMALL GRAY TRIANGLE
NOUN	BLACK EQUILATERAL - TRIANGLE
ADJECTIVE	BLUE EQUILATERAL
PRONOUN	PINK ISOCELE
VERB	RED CIRCLE
ADVERB	SMALLER ORANGE CIRCLE
CONJECTION	PURPLE/MAUVE BAR
PREPOSITION	GREEN (CRESCENT)
INTERJECTION	SUNNY YELLOW (SKITTLE SHAPE)

 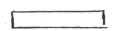

ARTICLE   PREPOSITION   INTERJECTION   CONJUNCTION

NOUN   VERB   ADJECTIVE   ADVERB   PRONOUN

Let's suppose that a passage in a book on American Indians consisted of the following:

The Indians of the Southwest lived in pueblos. These pueblos were made out of a sun-dried brick called adobe. Some of the pueblos were stacked one on top of another so that many people could live close together.

Now, you and your child must make simple sentences out of the passage so that he can easily determine the different parts of speech used. Explain to your child that what he and you are about to do is called "paraphrasing". This "paraphrasing" is done in conjunction with this grammar exercise and should not be used when he later writes reports for school work.

The first sentence of the above passage may be paraphrased in this manner.

The Southwest Indians lived in pueblos.

Remember, you child's sentences are going to seem simplistic to you at first. This is only natural. As he becomes more comfortable with writing sentences, you will see that he will use adverbs, adjectives and coordinating conjunctions more freely. Initially, though, he may be a little hesitant to use prepositions, adjectives, adverbs and coordinating conjunctions. Or, he may be so anxious to use the different parts of speech, that he uses them incorrectly. Do not criticize his efforts.

Gently point out his errors, while praising the other strong points about his sentences.

The second and third sentences of the preceding paragraphs about the Southwest Indians may be paraphrased by a first or second grader in the following manner:

The pueblos were made from brick. Some of the pueblos were stacked together.

Now, ask your child to tell you the parts of speech used in the first sentence. His answers should correspond with the following: The (article) Southwest (adjective) Indians (noun) lived (verb) in (preposition) pueblos (noun). Look at the picture on page 56. Notice how the symbols are used to label the different parts of speech.

After he has successfully completed identifying the parts of speech for the first sentence, encourage him to continue this exercise with the second and third sentences that he has written. He may enjoy saying aloud the part of speech as he places the appropriate symbol on top to the corresponding word.

The (article) pueblos (noun) were (helping verb) made (verb) from (preposition) brick (noun).

Some (adjective) of (preposition) the (article) pueblos (noun) were (helping verb) stacked (verb) together (adverb).

You can do this exercise with other sentences in the book. First, invite your child to paraphrase other passages. Then, use the grammar symbols to label the different parts of speech contained in the sentences. Select sentences that are short at first. Later, you may want to select sentences that contain conjunctions and/or prepositional phrases. Keep in mind that when your child paraphrases these sentences, they will undoubtedly shrink in size.

Now that your child is becoming proficient in writing sentences, you will want to help him prepare to write mini-reports. Encourage your child to write sentences relevant to his life. Perhaps he could write about his favorite pet, movie, amusement park, friend or relative.

When I teach or tutor I explain to the children that I am there to guide them, and, if I am knowledgeable about the topic, I will answer questions. The childrn know that I haven't abandoned them; moreover, when they finish their work, they have the satisfaction of knowing that "they" did it, and that I was just a tool to help them express themselves. You, too, will want to act as your child's "guide" through his first mini-report.

Narrowing the Topic

Once your child has chosen a topic, you can use the following example by just modifying it a bit. As an example, let's suppose that your child's favorite pet is his cat Rusty and that he has decided to write a mini-report about this adorable cat.

First, explain that every story or report has a beginning, where a thesis is presented to the reader, a middle, which consists of one or more paragraphs supporting the thesis presented in the first paragraph, and an ending, where the original thesis is restated and a conclusion is given. Of course, you can substitute the word "topic" for "thesis" when you talk to your child about writing a story. Later, when he writes scientific reports or comparative reports about art or music, you will want to use the word "thesis" exclusively.

Further explain to your child that the sentences that make up the beginning of his report should tell the reader his pet's name, color, possibly size, and so on. Later, when your child is in the third or fourth grade you can explain that these characteristics of the pet paint a picture in the reader's mind of what he is reading about.

Typically, the first or second grader will write something like this.

My favorite pet is my cat Rusty. He is eight years old and he is tan and white. He is the fattest cat that I have ever seen. He likes to play with me.

After your child has written an introduction, examine what he has written. Don't be critical. Even if there are numerous spelling errors or possibly grammar errors, refrain from criticizing his efforts. Remember, you want to keep the creativity flowing, so don't spoil it by making any negative comments at this point. Instead, focus on a sentence or "word" that may yield itself to further elaboration during the "middle" part of this mini-report.

In the example above the key sentence is as follows: **He likes to play with me.** This is not the only possible sentence that can be developed; however, it may be the most interesting one. A child six or seven would possibly develop it as follows.

He loves to play with ribbons and strings. At Christmas and on my birthday he plays with the ribbons and wrapping paper. He even helps me unwrap the gifts.

Notice that the word "play" is further developed in the middle part of this mini-report. *What* kind of play does the cat like to do? He chases ribbons and strings. *When?* On my birthday and at Christmas he plays with ribbons and wrapping paper.

Your job is to guide by asking questions. By asking where, how, and so on you help your child develop his key sentence.

As you know, the ending is a "summing up" of what the mini-report is about. Explain to your child that new information about the topic must not be introduced at this point.

Here is an example of an ending that a first or second grader might write for this topic.

I like coming home from school each day, because I know that we will have lots of fun together. Because we both like to play we will be friends forever.

The above example contains many choppy sentences. Absent is the continuity that is usually present in a mini-report done by a third or fourth grader. So don't expect a sophisticated mini-report from a typical first or second grader. There are some exceptional students who are gifted in composition, and this is apparent at a young age. However, in many children this gift may be latent. Obstacles like lack of concentration, lack of confidence, incorrect grammar, and the like may interfere with a child's writing ability, and it is not until these hurdles are overcome that we see the true talent that is there.

Reading – The Road to Increased Vocabulary Skills

Set a good example for your child by visiting your nearby library, at least twice a month. Borrow some books that you are interested in reading. Perhaps you and your child are considering growing certain flowers or vegetables. If you borrow a book on gardening, your child sees firsthand that the library is a useful tool for obtaining knowledge on a variety of subjects. He sees you thumb through the card catalog or search for the books you need by using the computer. As he glances around at the various books in the library, he may see a book that he may like to read. If the book contains reading material that is too difficult for him to understand, you and he can spend some time searching for a similar book on the same topic in the children's section. If you have difficulty locating it, he sees that either the children's librarian or reference librarian can provide the assistance that is needed. Therefore, this experience is educational in more ways than one.

If you borrow a book on gardening for yourself, you can suggest that your child borrow a book on plants. Be sure that the reading level of the book is appropriate for your child's ability, so that he won't be frustrated when he attempts to read it at home. Encourage your child to read the book on plants from cover to cover. Then, present an interesting science lesson by purchasing a packet of seeds, a pot and some planting soil.

When you present the lesson, use clear, concise instructions. Explain how the soil helps the seed grow. Your child will find the discussion of the nutrients in the soil and the role of water in the plant's growth and development fascinating if you use the CLASSIFIED READING CARDS shown on pages 65 and 66.

By studying these cards, your child learns the specific names for each part of the plant. Notice, that in each picture, a different area is darkened. When you make these cards at home, be sure to use a red pencil or red crayon to darken the areas. In Roots Picture 1 the root's area is darkened. In Picture 2 the stem area is darkened. In Picture 3 the leaves area is darkened. Finally, in Picture 4 the flower area is darkened. Remind your child that some plants have cones rather than flowers.

When you talk about a specific part of the plant with your child point to the picture where that area is darkened so that his attention will be focused upon it.

Explain to your child that a seed cannot become a plant unless it has a special environment in which to develop into its potential. Once planted and watered the seed receives nourishment from the soil. Now, place an index card with the word "roots" written on it, and place the card under the picture with the roots area shaded in red. Explain that the seed then grows into a young plant with roots which will insure constant nourishment. These roots are long spidery fingers that draw up moisture and nutrients from the soil.

This moisture and nourishment is carried up through the "stem" of the plant. Next, place the card with the word "stem" written on it under the picture of the stem shade in red. Explain that the stem is also important because it provides shape and support for the leaves. Now, place the card with "leaves" written on it under the picture with leaves shaded in red.

Further explain that the moisture that was drawn up from the roots through the stem now reaches the "leaves". Direct your child's attention to the picture of the leaves shaded in red.

Further explain, that the leaves make food for the plant. Finally, draw your child's attention to the flower. Explain to your child that the flower is where seeds are formed. Thus, the cycle begins again.

You may want to spend a little time talking about how plants use sunlight to convert energy, but I would strongly discourage a detailed discussion of photosynthesis at this point. You have to consider your child's level of understanding, attention span and other variables, i.e. his interest, when planning a scientific presentation. Remember, you want your child to look forward to each learning session. If the material presented is too difficult for him to comprehend, he may feel frustrated and inadequate.

Reading and the Social Sciences

Notice how your child's vocabulary has increased from that one science lesson alone. He has learned the scientific terms that relate to plants. However, you want your child's vocabulary to be well rounded so that he feels comfortable talking about and relating to varied educational topics.

Therefore, it is important for him to read many books on a variety of subjects.

If your child enjoyed reading about Indians, you may consider having him select additional books on this subject. You may then want to discuss what he has read. For example, you may ask him to tell you how the Indians of the Great Plains differ from the Indians of the Southwest. He should be able to tell you the differences in their diet, housing and mode of transportation. By asking questions in a relaxed, happy setting, your child has the satisfaction of sharing with you what he has read. Your discussions also help him to increase his reading comprehension.

To make this lesson in social studies even more enjoyable, you may suggest that he make an art project using some of the materials that the Indians used. My project consists of using leather figures and beads plus a list of codes of written symbols that Indians used to communicate. The materials for this project can be purchased by mail order from **The Indian Store** which is located in Anaheim, California. You will find the address for **The Indian Store** on page 146 of this book.

Indian Art Project

BEAVER

HOGAN

BEAVER TAIL

INDIAN CAMP

HOUSE

CORN

HEART

WHITE HAWK

BIRD TRACKS

NOON

CANOE

SUNRISE

FISH

SNAKES

WAR

CHILD

DAYS & NIGHTS

RAIN

SNOW

MOON & STARS
SHINING BRIGHT

TURKEY

STRONG

73

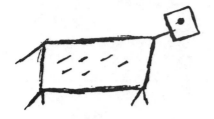

JOURNEY

FISH

RIVER

ARROWHEAD
ALERTNESS

CHIEF

SUN RAYS
CONSTANCY

DESERT

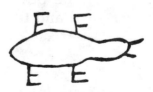

GILA MONSTER
SIGN OF THE DESERT

The children are each given a leather disc that is 2 1/2" in diameter. Two holes near the top of the leather disc are punched out with a leather puncher. However, if you purchase the disc from **The Indian Store** you will not encounter this problem. The discs are sold with the holes already punched out. On the smooth surface of the disc, the child may select any of the written symbols that appear on pages 71-74 of this book. Once he has selected the written symbol(s) he wishes to put on the disc, he uses an ink pen or pencil to draw the symbol on the disc.

Next, the child gets a piece of leather or plastic string which is about 1/8" wide and 8" long. The child then laces this leather or plastic string through the two holes near the top of the disc. Next, the child selects eight beads to string through the leather pieces. Four beads are strung on one side and the other four are strung on the opposite side. A knot is made on each side to hold the beads in place. Finally, the piece of leather is tied into two knots at the top. The child has now made' a key chain which can be given to either his mother, father or some other friend or relative. The knots can be untied and the keys can be slipped into place and then the recipient can retie the piece of leather or plastic string into two knots.

If you are interested in some additional Indian projects I strongly suggest that you contact **The Indian Store** in person, by phone or by mail.

Here is a sampling of what you'll find there:

LEATHER FIGURES
Large Disc 3"
Small Disc 2"
Indian Chief Head
Kachina
Spear Point
Arrowhead
Tipi
War Skirt
Buffalo
Bear
Thunderbird
Fox/Wolf/Coyote

LACES
1/8" Cowhide (copper)
1/8" Boot Lace (colors)
1/8" Boot Lace (beige)
Plastic Lace (color)
Imitation Sinew

BEADS
Crow Beads
Tube Beads
Wood Beads
Plastic Eagle Claws
Plastic Bear Claws
Large Plastic Claws
Plastic Arrowheads
Plastic Elk & Buffalo Teeth

FEATHERS
Tips (approx. 2")
Fluff (3'-6")
Flat Fluff (3"-6")
Quills (colors)
Quills (imitation eagle
  brown/black tip
Quills (separate)

VEST KITS
Split cowhide, copper color,
instructions and vest ties
included

COPPER COWBELLS
Small (1")
Medium (2")
Large (3")

KITS
Regular Bonnet
Mid Length Bonnet
Full Length Bonnet

Poetry & Grammar - A Winning Combination

Longfellow eloquently captured the true meaning of the pictorial symbols that the Indians used in his poem "Hiawatha". If your child is in the second grade he may enjoy reading this poem aloud. If your child is in the first grade be sure to read this poem to him. He will revel in the rhythm and imagery that the poem provides. Point out to your child how Longfellow used adverbs and adjectives to paint a picture in the reader's mind, i.e. the black and gloomy pine trees, firs with cones upon them, clear and sunny water, stars that shine in heaven, fiery tresses, the firefly, twinkling of its candle and lighting up the brakes and brushes.

Spend time discussing this legendary chieftain named Hiawatha. In particular, discuss what life in the 1500's may have been like. Describe to your child how Indians belonged to different tribes and that what is sometimes shown on television is fiction, not an accurate portrayal of what Indian life was really like.

Hiawatha was said to have been an active force of the Iroquois tribe. Much credit has been given to him for developing the union of the Five Nations. As you know, the Five Nations served to protect the Iroquois against the more aggressive Algonquin tribe. American children should be made aware of the contributions that the American Indians have made, and by reading the poem "Hiawatha" in addition to the many books listed on page 151 of this book, they will more fully appreciate the First Americans.

Discovering the World

You may have used a map of the United States when discussing the American Indians with your child. Undoubtedly, your child was a little amazed at the size and shape of the United States. He probably was a little surprised that we share this continent with Canada, Mexico and Central America, for young children find it difficult to conceptualize this at first. However, Maria Montessori felt that children should be familiar with the geography of the world and she devised materials which would help children recognize the differences in the size and shape of the various continents.

Matching Continent Cards

One exercise, the MATCHING CONTINENT CARDS, pictured on page 110 of this book, is relatively simple and inexpensive to make. Purchase 14 – 8 1/2" x 11" sheets of beige or white construction paper or lightweight posterboard. On seven of the fourteen sheets draw a continent i.e. one for South America, one for North America, one for Antarctica, one for Australia, one for Europe, one for Asia and one for Africa. If you can't or don't like to draw, then trace these continents on to the construction paper.

Make seven identical continent cards as companions to the first set that you made. You will then have two identical Africa continent cards, two identical Asia continent cards, and so on.

Use the Three Period Lesson to introduce this exercise to your child. For example, you should only present three continent cards at a time, i.e. Africa, Asia, Europe. Later, add a continent card, one at a time, so as not to confuse your child.

Your child may want to color the continents different colors and this should be encouraged. Often, the continent and countries are color coded on world globes, so you may want to spend some time showing your child where the different continents are. Later, he may want to locate them himself. Your child will undoubtly have many questions involving the climate, animals, customs and, of course people living in other parts of the world, so be prepared for some interesting discussions! Your first grader will enjoy matching the continent cards on his own, and this should be encouraged.

Vocabulary and Foreign Languages

The United States has become a melting pot of people, rich with diversity of language and culture. Think for a moment of the changes in the population of the United States during the last twenty years or so. Undoubtedly, there will continue to be an influx of people from different countries entering the United States, and your child will most likely encounter many people speaking other languages than his own native tongue during the next ten years. Therefore, you may consider exposing your child now, to other foreign languages, rather than waiting until he is a freshman in high school.

Many private Montessori schools offer instruction in a foreign language, and the children are delighted to learn in such a setting because the environment is often properly prepared. If Spanish is taught, one room is prepared for the instruction, complete with Spanish decor, Spanish music, various posters in Spanish, and a Spanish calendar. Often the children are encouraged to help in the preparation of a Spanish meal. In many instances, the instruction is presented by a native Spanish speaking individual.

For example, while teaching the children to make a beef enchilada the teacher uses simple commands, asking for ingredients in Spanish. The children then learn that (carne) is the equivalent to beef (el queso) is equivalent to cheese, and so on.

Perhaps you know of a person who speaks fluent Spanish, French, Italian, Chinese, Korean or whatever language you and your child are interested in learning more about. Inquire as to whether this person would be willing to take the time to instruct your child in this language.

Observe how this person and your child interact. If the instructor is not patient or makes your child feel dumb, the lessons will be frustrating for your child and unrewarding for you. Moreover, if your child feels that he is not yet ready to study another language, you may have to intervene and discontinue the lessons.

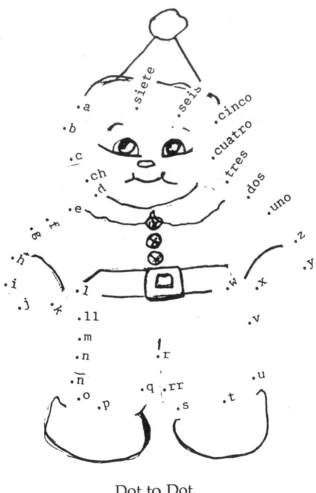

Dot to Dot

1. The Name of the Country below the United States

2. Another name for City

3. Spanish name for Miss

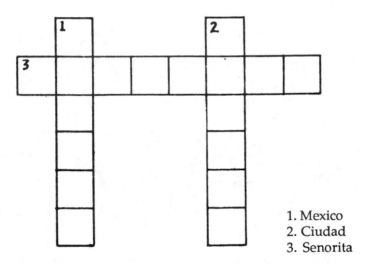

1. Mexico
2. Ciudad
3. Senorita

Be aware that some children are afraid to fail; therefore, they simply say that they are not ready to learn something new, when in fact, the fear of failure impedes their efforts. If your child is less than confident about studying a new language, reassure him with approval for <u>any</u> progress that he makes and encourage him to continue to try if he is willing. Montessori felt that it was imperative that the child be totally involved in the language process. If his "will" is involved true learning will occur; if his "will" is not involved, both you and he are wasting time.

If your child is enthusiastic about learning another language you may inquire about supplemental exercises that he can do at home. You do not necessarily have to be fluent in the language to assist with these supplemental exercises. For example, if your child is learning Spanish, you can make a crossword puzzle, matching cards and dot-to-dot exercises that will help reinforce what was learned during his formal lessons with the instructor.

Use the Spanish alphabet to create a dot-to-dot exercise for your child like the one pictured on page 81. For the matching cards exercise, you can either purchase some preschool matching cards and then print the Spanish name for each picture or make matching cards yourself. For example, if the set of preschool matching cards has two pictures of a dog print two labels that say (el perro) and place over the English equivalent (the dog).

You can also take the vocabulary list that the instructor has given your child to study and use it to create exciting crossword puzzles for your child. See page 82.

If your child is studying German, French, Italian, or Spanish use the Grammar Parsing Trays to help him recognize the parts of speech. The possibilities are endless. Do a little brainstorming on your own to devise some exercises that you know your child would enjoy!

Chapter 5
CREATIVE TEACHING FOR
THIRD AND FOURTH GRADERS

Now that your child has become more proficient in reading and writing, more avenues than ever are open to him. If your child is a reluctant reader, you may try scheduling a few field trips to whet his appetite for wanting to know more about a given subject. For example, if you live in the Southern California area plan a visit to the **Natural History Museum** in Los Angeles. This large museum houses an exquisite rock, mineral, and gem collection, Americana memorabilia, a dinosaur exhibit, marine life exhibit and a botany exhibit to name a few. Luckily, the **California Museum of Science and Industry** is housed next door and many people go to both museums during one visit.

People living in the eastern part of the United States have a plethora of museums to see. In the state of Massachusetts your family can visit the **Berkshire Museum, Museum of Fine Arts Boston** and **Museum of Science** to name a few. If you live in the Washington, D.C. area, you and your child are in for a real treat. This city is full of history, and even the reluctant reader is bound to leave this city with a thirst for more knowledge about our forefathers or American history in general.

Virtually every state in the union has something magnificent to offer. If you live in the midwest and plan to visit another part of the country, write for a tourist's guide. Once you get the guide, make a note of sites that you know that your child would enjoy seeing. If you will be travelling by car or by train you may want to obtain information about the states that you will be passing through on the way to your destination. Once again, the library often has books on each of the individual states in the union, so you may want to conduct some of your research there.

If you live on the east or west coast and are planning a vacation to one of the midwestern states, the preceding suggestions may be of benefit to you as well. Besides prestigious universities and a plentiful amount of museums, the midwestern states have something special to offer. These states are rich with information about agriculture and

86

livestock. Visit the county fair and talk with the exhibitors. This will be like a field trip for your child. He will learn much by talking with the experts. Moreover, your child will love seeing and touching the farm animals. Spend some time driving through the towns so that your child will see the beauty of the countryside. It is one thing to envision what the countryside is like by reading a book about it, and another to actually experience it.

Whether your child is a reluctant reader or has an insatiable appetite for reading, you will soon see that educational experiences like the above have a profound effect upon him. Often, when he reads a story or does some research for a project on a topic that he is familiar with, he can readily identify with it. *Why?* Because you have encouraged him to learn about different types of people, places and things. You have discouraged him from living in his own little microcosm. Rather, you have given him the tools to becoming a self-actualized human being.

Reading for General Knowledge

Now is the time to prepare your child for the SAT or ACT. A few years ago when I was tutoring high school students for the American College Testing Program and the Scholastic Aptitude test, I became somewhat frustrated at times because I couldn't give these students all of the assistance that they needed. The longer I worked with these students the more I realized that their difficulties stemmed from a lack of general knowledge and poor vocabulary skills. These students were bright, but they thought that reading was boring. They read only when they **had** to.

Therefore, I implemented some general knowledge and vocabulary strengthening exercises that I am about to share with you. Obviously, because of their advanced reading ability and need for advanced vocabulary skills the process was longer and more involved than what I am covering in this book.

First, acquaint your child with the classics. Perhaps your child is an avid reader who is reading at the fourth grade level or advanced third grade level. If so, I would strongly suggest that you purchase a set of classics by *PLAYMORE, Inc*. These books are sold in a set of twelve. The set I purchased at Sears for third and fourth grade students included the following titles:

THE WIZARD OF OZ
TREASURE ISLAND
HEIDI
AROUND THE WORLD IN EIGHTY DAYS
A CONNECTICUT YANKEE IN
    KING ARTHUR'S COURT
THE THREE MUSKETEERS
KIDNAPPED
BLACK BEAUTY
THE ADVENTURES OF ROBINSON CRUSOE
SHERLOCK HOLMES
20,000 LEAGUES UNDER THE SEA
LITTLE WOMEN

Some of these titles may not appeal to your child. Moreover, some children are very sensitive and science fiction stories are upsetting to them. I am somewhat hesitant to let my third or fourth grade students read science fiction material; however, I realize that some may not share my views. Overall, I feel that the *PLAYMORE, Inc.* series is an excellent beginning classics series.

Your child may also enjoy the *LADYBIRD BOOKS*. These books are beautifully illustrated and well written. Some of the titles available include:

TALES OF KING ARTHUR
   MYSTERIES OF MERLIN
   DEEDS OF THE NAMELESS KNIGHT
   SIR LANCELOT OF THE LAKE
   THE KNIGHT OF THE GOLDEN FALCON

ROBIN HOOD ADVENTURES
   ROBIN HOOD OUTLAWED
   ROBIN HOOD AND THE KING'S RANSOM
   ROBIN HOOD TO THE RESCUE
   ROBIN HOOD AND THE SILVER ARROW

LADYBIRD CHILDREN'S CLASSICS
   GULLIVER'S TRAVELS
   TREASURE ISLAND
   SWISS FAMILY ROBINSON
   THE SECRET GARDEN
   A JOURNEY TO THE CENTRE OF THE EARTH
   THE THREE MUSKETEERS
   A TALE OF TWO CITIES
   THE LOST WORLD

Many United States bookstores will order these books for you. For additional ordering information see page 145.

If your child can't stand the thought of reading the classics then the **ILLUSTRATED CLASSICS** by **PENDULUM PRESS** may be the answer. These books are cleverly illustrated to capture the young reader's attention. Some of the titles include:

BLACK BEAUTY
THE CALL OF THE WILD
HUCKLEBERRY FINN
MOBY DICK
THE RED BADGE OF COURAGE
THE TIME MACHINE
TOM SAWYER
TREASURE ISLAND
20,000 LEAGUES UNDER THE SEA
GULLIVER'S TRAVEL
JOURNEY TO THE CENTRE OF THE EARTH
KIDNAPPED
THE MYSTERIOUS ISLAND
THE STORY OF MY LIFE
A TALE OF TWO CITIES
THE THREE MUSKETEERS
THE WAR OF THE WORLDS
AROUND THE WORLD IN EIGHTY DAYS
CAPTAINS COURAGEOUS
A CONNECTICUT YANKEE IN
    KING ARTHUR'S COURT
JANE EYRE
THE LAST OF THE MOHICANS
TWO YEARS BEFORE THE MAST
WHITE FANG
WUTHERING HEIGHTS
BEN HUR
A CHRISTMAS CAROL

IVANHOE
THE PRINCE AND THE PAUPER
ROBINSON CRUSOE
THE SEA WOLF
THE SWISS FAMILY ROBINSON
DON QUIXOTE
HEIDI
GREAT EXPECTATIONS
THE ILIAD
THE MUTINY ON BOARD H.M.S. BOUNTY
OLIVER TWIST
PRIDE AND PREJUDICE
JULIUS CAESAR BY SHAKESPEARE
ROMEO AND JULIET BY SHAKESPEARE

Because many of these stories are action packed, many fifth and sixth graders thrive on these **PENDULUM ILLUSTRATED** books as well.

Beginning readers as well as reluctant third and fourth grade readers will like the **KIDS' CLASSICS EASY-READING LIBRARY** by *Lakeshore Curriculum Materials Company*. The sentences are easy to read and the illustrations add excitement to the stories. Some of the titles include:

TOM SAWYER
OLIVER TWIST
TREASURE ISLAND
GULLIVER'S TRAVELS
and many more . . .

Re-read these classics yourself so that you can discuss the content of each book with your child. Some of the classics are set in different time periods; thus, your child will receive valuable history lessons as well. If he seems interested in a certain time period, encourage him to learn more about it by borrowing history books from the library. Moreover, encyclopedias provide a wealth of information on numerous topics, so encourage him to continue to use this valuable resource as well.

Some of these classics for beginning readers may be available at the local library, so you may want to check with your reference librarian. If your child enjoys reading books written by a particular author, you may want to encourage him to ask the librarian if the author has written more than one book. If your child has received instruction on how to use the card catalog or computer, he will be able to locate this information for himself.

Vocabulary - Word Building Exercises

EXAMPLES OF VOCABULARY BUILDING PREFIXES, SUFFIXES AND ROOTS FOR THIRD AND FOURTH GRADERS

PREFIX	WORDS CONTAINING PREFIX
PRE (Before)	PREFIX, PREMATURE, PREFACE, PREVIEW
AB (Away from)	ABNORMAL, ABSOLVE
RE (Again)	RECHARGE, RENEW
BI (Two)	BICEPS, BICENTENNIAL, BICYCLE, BILINGUAL
TRI (Three)	TRICEPS, TRICYCLE
UN (Not)	UNHAPPY, UNSCRAMBLE

ROOTS

GEO (Earth)	GEOGRAPHY, GEOLOGY, GEOCENTRIC
BIO (Life)	BIOLOGY, BIOGRAPHY
DERM (Skin)	DERMIS, DERMATOLOGY
CARD (Heart)	CARDIOLOGIST, CARDIOLOGY
ASTR (Star)	ASTRONAUT, ASTRONOMER

SUFFIXES

MENT (State of being)	ENJOYMENT, GOVERNMENT
LY (Like)	NICELY, SWEETLY
NESS (State of being)	CARELESSNESS, COMPLETENESS
ITIS (Inflammation)	DERMATITIS, CARDITIS, LARYNGITIS

Before your child tackles these exercises, he should be able to easily decode words. If he is experiencing difficulty in the area of phonics, the exercises discussed in Chapter IV should be reviewed. Some children like to practice these exercises periodically to strengthen their skills, and this should be encouraged. Montessori noticed that children like to repeat an enjoyable activity many times because of the new insight they receive each time it is repeated.

93

Prefixes should be presented in the same manner that you presented the phonograms to your child. Review Chapter IV of this book if necessary to determine how to construct Prefix Bingo. Follow the directions for Phonogram Bingo. However, instead of making phonogram cards, you will be making prefix cards. You will want to make prefix cards for *re, de, un,* and *in* to name a few. Then, as you did for Phonogram Bingo and for the other phonogram exercises, make corresponding cards in different colors for each of the prefix headings. For example, if you have used the color blue to denote all prefixes under the "un" category words like unhappy, unreal, unlike and uncertain would be written on blue index cards, one word per card. Words with the prefix "in" like inside, inactive, and inept would be written on a different colored card, i.e. pink or yellow.

You may also want to construct a Suffix Bingo Game and a Roots Bingo Game. Examples of suffixes, prefixes and roots are listed on page 93 for your convenience.

Present the words on page 93 in conjunction with a thesaurus exercise. The Suffix, Prefix and Roots Bingo Games will be more meaningful if your child is able to understand the meaning of the words on his game card. If you don't own a thesaurus, borrow one from your local library.

Encourage your child to find words that have the same prefix as the word he is studying. Use the list words on pages 92-93 for some initial examples.

Explain how the synonyms and antonyms relate to the word he is studying. Present only a few words at a time. For example, if your child is studying the prefix "pre" you may want to present the words "prefix". "premature" and "preface" during one learning session.

Some children love working with a thesaurus. Others despise working with it at first. If your child resists the idea of using this tool, guide him to another excellent implement, the dictionary. He probably has used one at school; however, you may want to purchase a beginner's dictionary for home use.

Once your child has become familiar with the structure and function of prefixes, roots and suffixes in word building, move on to showing him how the process works by using concrete examples.

Science and Vocabulary Building

You will find a liberal use of Latin and Greek prefixes, roots and suffixes in the world of science. The field of health, in particular, provides the third and fourth grader with a unique opportunity to concurrently increase his general knowledge of science while practicing vocabulary building.

Children are often exposed to the study of health during the third and fourth grades. Some public school districts and private schools include health in their second grade curriculum as well. Therefore, plan now to give your child an introduction to the study of health so that he will feel relaxed and enthusiastic if he encounters this subject in a school setting.

Borrow some books from the library on human anatomy and physiology, health and disease. See Appendix D for some examples. Become familiar with the anatomy and physiology of the various systems, i.e. cardiovascular, respiratory, digestive and so forth. Then make a diagram of the system or organ that you plan to present to your child. For example, if you plan to present a lecture on the circulation of blood through the heart you may want to draw a diagram like the one shown on pages 99-106.

Next, xerox eight copies of it. On each diagram darken a different area of the heart so that your child's attention will be focused upon it. You may want to refer to the diagram of the plant on pages 65 and 66 of this book. Notice that different parts of the plant are darkened in each of the four pictures. This time, you will repeat this process using the diagram of the circulation of the blood through the heart rather than the parts of the plant.

The Blood's Journey through the Heart

You may want to explain the diagram on page 99 in the following manner. Initially, explain to your child that the right and left sides are reversed on anatomical drawings. So that what looks like areas on the left side of the drawing are actually on the right and vice versa. Explain to your child that what he is looking at is the primary organ responsible for the blood's circulation. Further, explain that this portion of the heart is responsible for the systemic blood flow for the entire body.

Next, step-by-step go through the diagram with him. Explain to your child that there are four chambers of the heart. The upper chambers are called the atria and the lower chambers are called the ventricles. Then, direct your child's attention to the inferior and superior vena cava. See Diagram 1. Explain that the blood which has traveled from the upper body portion, i.e. head and arms and from the lower portion, trunk and legs, is carried to the heart by the superior and inferior vena cava. The blood then meets in the right atrium as shown in Diagram 2. This blood is full of CO_2, Carbon Dioxide. Blood then travels to the right ventricle as illustrated in Diagram 3. From there the blood goes to each pulmonary artery. See Diagram 4. Notice that there are two pulmonary arteries, one pulmonary artery for the left lung and one for the right lung. In the lungs there is a gaseous exchange of CO_2, Carbon dioxide for O_2, Oxygen. Explain to your child that each time he exhales he breathes out this waste material, CO_2, and when he in inhales he provides his lungs with a fresh source of O_2. However, the actual exchange takes place in tiny air sacs in the lungs. These air sacs are called alveoli. The blood, now rich in O_2, enters the pulmonary veins as illustrated in Diagram 5. Again, notice that there are two veins, one carrying the blood from the left lung and one carrying blood from the right lung. The blood the meets in the left atrium as shown in

Diagram 6. From there, then blood goes down to the left ventricle and out through the aorta. See Diagram 7. Notice that there is an ascending aorta and a descending aorta. The ascending aorta carries blood to the head and arms area and the descending aorta carries blood to the trunk and legs area. Once again, every cell in the body receives a fresh supply of O_2.

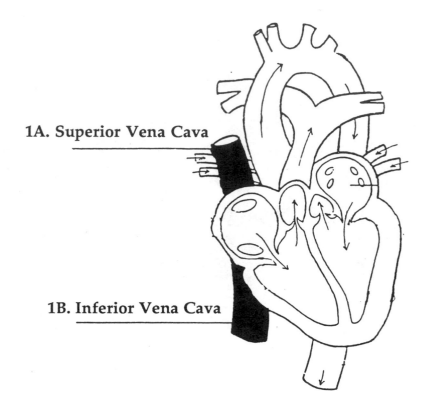

1A. Superior Vena Cava

1B. Inferior Vena Cava

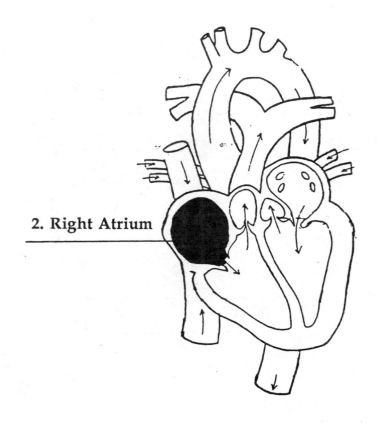

2. Right Atrium

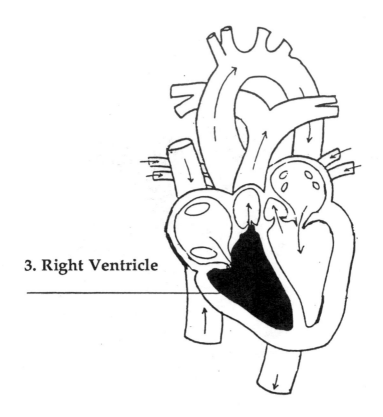

3. Right Ventricle

4. Pulmonary Arteries

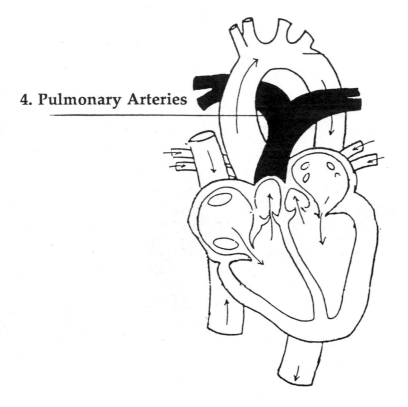

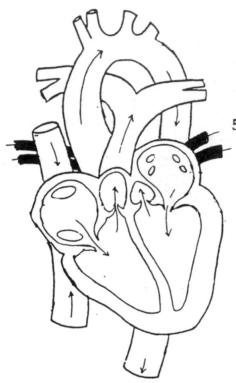

5. Pulmonary Veins

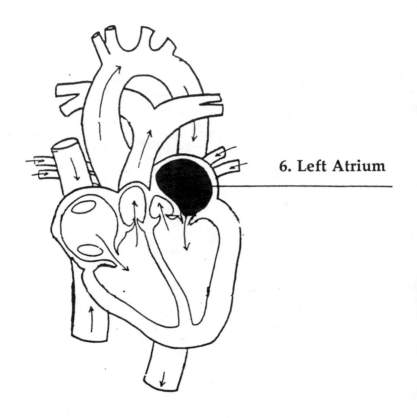

6. Left Atrium

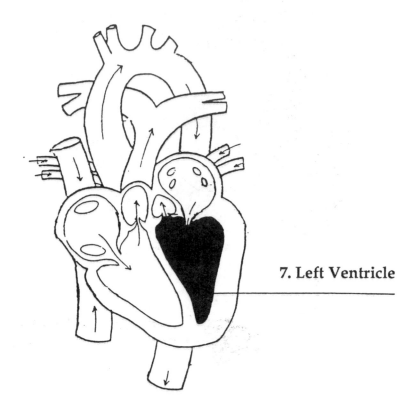

7. Left Ventricle

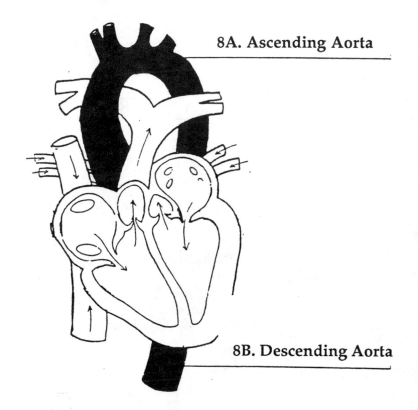

8A. Ascending Aorta

8B. Descending Aorta

Obviously, the preceding discussion has been presented in a simplistic manner so that a third or fourth grader can more fully appreciate the heart's function. Hopefully, this discussion will interest your child in learning more about the terminology used when discussing the heart's function.

I have selected appropriate cardiac terms that your third or fourth grader may enjoy learning. Dissecting these words gives your child practice in word building. Moreover, learning the meaning of these words increases his vocabulary and, in particular, his general knowledge. Encourage your child to look up the words blood, heart, and lungs in his encyclopedia. Then, invite him to write three or four sentences, using his own words, about what he has learned.

SELECTED HEART TERMS

WORD	MEANING
ANOXIA	WITHOUT OXYGEN (AN=WITHOUT OX=OXYGEN)
ARTERITIS	INFLAMMATION OF ARTERIES (ITIS = INFLAMMATION OF ARTER = ARTERIES)
CARDIAC	HAVING TO DO WITH THE HEART (CARD = HEART)
CARDIOLOGY	THE STUDY OF THE HEART (CARD = HEART LOGY= STUDY OF)
HEMOGLOBIN	OXYGEN CARRYING RED BLOOD CELLS (HEMO=BLOOD) (GLOB=ROUND)
HYPERTENSION	HIGH BLOOD PRESSURE (HYPER = HIGH TENSION = PRESSURE)
HYPOTENSION	LOW BLOOD PRESSSURE (HYPO=LOW TENSION=PRESSURE)
PHLEBITIS	INFLAMMATION OF A VEIN (PHLEB = VEIN ITIS = INFLAMMATION OF)

Adventures in Geography

The Classified Reading Cards exercise can be creatively used to stimulate your child's interest in learning more about the United States and the world in general. First, purchase 14 sheets of either white construction paper or white lightweight posterboard. Next, using a black marking pen, draw each of the seven continents on the sheets of posterboard or construction paper, i.e. one sheet for South America, one sheet for North America, one sheet for Antarctica, one sheet for Africa, one sheet for Asia, one sheet for Europe and one sheet for Australia. Then, make an identical mate for each of the seven so that you have seven pairs or fourteen completed sheets. (See page 110).

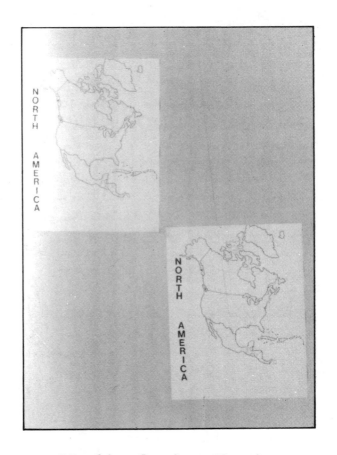

Matching Continent Exercise

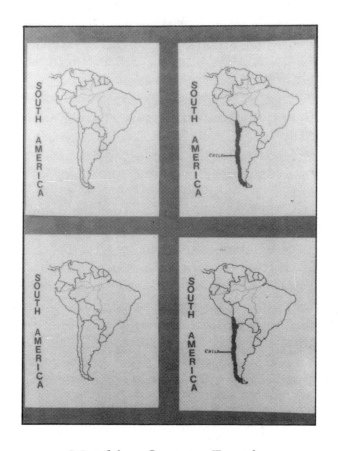

Matching Country Exercise

You will want to draw authentic representations of these continents, complete with lines of demarcation for the borders of the different countries and states in each continent. Therefore, these drawings will seem more sophisticated than the ones mentioned in Chapter IV of this book.

When you initially present this exercise to your child, you will only use three pairs. For example, during the first learning session you may wish to present the continents of Asia, Africa and Australia. If you presented the previous exercise mentioned in Chapter IV to your child he should be able to easily identify them. Once again, ask him to show you where they are located on the world globe. If your child experiences no difficulty matching the first three pairs of continents proceed on to the presentation of the remaining continents and give him ample time to practice matching the continents.

However, if your child is experiencing some difficulty, or if you did not present the exercise in Chapter IV to your child then continue as follows. First, show your child where the continent, i.e. Asia, is on a world map or globe so that he sees its position in relationship to other countries, oceans and so on. Next, present the illustration of Asia that you drew for him. Then, request that he find its mate. This will be quite easy for the third or fourth grader to do. Impress upon him, however, that he should make a mental note of its outline so that he can readily identify it later on during another learning session. Continue in this manner with Africa and Australia.

During your next learning session together you may want to present the other four continents, using the same method you used to present Asia, Africa, and Australia. Or, you may want to review the first three continents and only introduce two additional sets.

If your child likes flash cards, you can use the drawings to reinforce what your child has learned before proceeding on to the next step. Some children love working with flash cards, while others feel pressured and anxious. Remember, learning the continents should not be an exercise in memorization. Rather, you want your child to appreciate the formation of continents, climate in the different sections of each continent, the culture and customs of the inhabitants of each continent and so forth. Therefore, encourage your child to learn more about these continents by researching them at the library or by using his encyclopedias. In addition, your child will undoubtedly enjoy reading some of the selected books mentioned in Appendix E of this book.

Once your child has learned to identify the seven continents focus his attention upon the individual countries in each continent. In many of the Montessori schools, Classified Reading Cards and Matching Cards exercises are used to help the child locate and recognize individual continents and countries. Therefore, I strongly suggest that you

113

use this technique when you present geography to your child as well.

Present only three countries of a given continent during a learning session. As an example, notice that I have chosen to illustrate the country Chile in the diagram on page 111. I have also made an identical mate so that a child can easily make a match. Using the Classified Reading Cards technique I have darkened only the country of Chile. That way a child's attention is focused upon it.

To save time, you will want to xerox multiple copies of South America, two for each of the countries, plus some extra ones in case errors are made. Darken the country of Chile on two of your South America illustrations. On another two of your South America illustrations darken another country, i.e. Brazil. Continue in this manner until you have made three sets. Your child will then be able to match the illustrations of Chile, the illustrations of Brazil and so forth.

Geography and Postage Stamps

The typical third or fourth grade student likes to collect things like stickers, rocks, baseball cards and *postage* stamps! Therefore, you can create some stimulating geography lessons for your child by purchasing a 22" x 28" map of the world, a 22" x 28" map of the United States and some used postage stamps. These maps sell for about $1.25 each, which is about the price of one sheet of white posterboard. However, if you love to draw, purchase a sheet of white lightweight posterboard and draw the United States on one side and a map of the world on the reverse side.

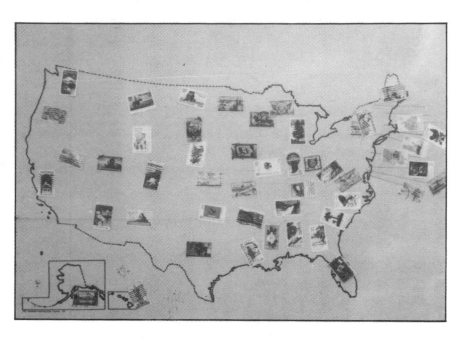

If you are fortunate enough to have a stamp and coin shop near by, stop in and discuss the geography project with the owner. Explain that you are interested in purchasing a packet of canceled postage stamps from all over the world so that your child can glue the stamps on to the world map. Further explain that you also need separate state stamps for each state in the United States so that your child will learn where the states on the map are located. The owner may direct you to small containers of used stamps and invite you to select the stamps that you wish to purchase. Since this is quite time consuming, you may want to purchase some of the stamps during one visit and enlist your child to help you during subsequent visits.

Your child will undoubtedly be fascinated with the variety of stamps that he encounters while searching for stamps from different countries. Stamps, after all, are quite educational. Be prepared to have some interesting discussions with your child about history, music and art to name a few. Perhaps your child will decide to collect stamps. He may wish to only collect topical stamps, i.e. of dogs, cats, or of the Olympics to name a few. Or, he may choose to collect stamps on a variety of different topics. Either way, he is bound to increase his general knowledge by pursuing this hobby. **The Stamps & Coins Shop** located in Anaheim, California is an excellent place to visit for either the novice or connoisseur. The owner and his personnel are friendly; moreover, because the selection is so comprehensive you will find many things that you need during one visit.

If you don't live in Southern California and won't be visiting in the near future, you may want to consider writing to **The Stamps & Coins Shop** for more information about their prices. Be specific in your letter and state the quantity of stamps wanted, types of stamps desired and so on. For the address of **The Stamps & Coins Shop** see page 146.

The Magic Formula:
Stamps + Pen Pals + Geography = Fun

One inexpensive way for your child to collect stamps, learn more about geography and improve his written English is to correspond with a pen pal. I used the Student Letter Exchange which was headquartered in Austin, Minnesota a few years ago and was very pleased with the results. For a nominal fee your child can request names of pen pals from the United States as well as from abroad. Most of the pen pals abroad were between the ages of nine and twelve, but my students didn't mind the age difference.

One way to insure that your child's experience with a pen pal is a positive one is to adhere to the following guidelines. First, encourage your child to select names of three pen pals he wishes to correspond with. Keep in mind that if a pen pal has found someone else to correspond with before your child's letter arrives, the pen pal will probably ignore your child's letter. Another unfortunate possibility is that if a pen pal has moved and left no forwarding address, your child's letter will probably be returned to your house. If a forwarding address was given to the post office, the pen pal may respond. However, his response may not arrive for many months. Therefore, if your child writes an introductory letter to three pen pals his chances of a reply are significantly increased.

Second, encourage your child to write a neat, well organized, interesting introductory letter. Stress that the appearance and contents of the letter will have some bearing on whether a pen pal writes a reply letter.

You may want to review with your child the parts of a letter, i.e., heading, greeting, body, closing and signature.

HEADING:

> 345 Crescent Avenue
> Long Beach, CA 90000

SALUTATION:
Dear Judy,

BODY:
Hi! My name is Melanie. I am 9 years old. I have two brothers. Both of them are older than I am. My brother Scott attends Michael Prescott High School. My brother Tim attends the University of Southern California. He wants to become a dentist.

I attend Parker Avenue School. I like most of the subjects that I study, but my favorite is art. I love to draw. I also enjoy swimming, bike riding, stamp collecting, roller skating and reading mystery books.

What are your favorite hobbies? Do you enjoy reading? If so, what types of books do you enjoy reading?

My father visited Australia two years ago, and he said that it was as beautiful as ever. My grandfather and uncle still live in Australia, and when they write to me, they enclose picture postcards. I look forward to receiving them, because with each picture, I see a little more of your beautiful country.

Please write and tell me about your school, friends and family. I hope to receive a reply from you very soon!

CLOSING

CLOSING

Your new friend,

SIGNATURE

Stacey Wellington

Third, have your child ask questions that will give the pen pal an opportunity to discuss what his family, hobbies, school and so on are like.

The letter on page 118 is typical of the introductory letter that many of my students have written. You may want to use it as a guideline.

If your child is studying a foreign language encourage him to choose a pen pal from a corresponding country where the language is spoken. Because many of my students study Spanish, I suggest selecting pen pals from countries like Mexico, Spain, Brazil, Argentina, Chile and so on. Then, I encourage my students to write bilingual letters to the individual. In most instances, the pen pal is learning English and appreciates the opportunity to read a bilingual letter. He has the opportunity to practice reading English, and my student has the practice of corresponding in Spanish. When my student receives the reply letter he receives practice in reading Spanish. The body of the letter may look something like this:

Me llamo Maria. My name is Maria.

Soy de Canada. I am from Canada.

Vivo en California. I live in California.

Vivo con mi familia. I live with my family.

Tengo una hermana. I have one sister.

Se llama Angela. Para sus amigos, se llama Angie.
Her name is Angela. But her friends call her Angie.

Estudio español. Angie estudia espanol tambien.
I am studying Spanish. Angie is studying Spanish too.

Me gusta escuchar música popular.
I like listening to popular music.

Me gusta tocar el piano y el clarinete.
I like to play the piano and clarinet.

¿Que instrumento toca Usted? What instrument do you play?

¿Que estudias ahora? What are you studying now?

¿Tiene usted hermanos y hermanas?
Do you have brothers and sisters?

120

Your child may receive a reply letter like the following. Notice that the pen pal opted to write the entire letter first in English and then in Spanish. The names have been changed to protect the students' privacy; however, the rest of the contents remains unchanged. You will notice that the pen pal made some errors in English. Remind your child that the pen pal is just learning to speak and write English. Moreover, your child may make some mistakes when he writes to his foreign pen pal, too.

EXAMPLE OF ACTUAL BILINGUAL LETTER FROM PEN PAL

Dear Maria,

(sic)

It was pretty nice the stickers you put on my letter. I think it is good to collect stickers. I collect stickers and postal stickers.

I like school only on Fridays because we don't have homework and sometimes we leave school at 12:00 p.m. Normally we leave school at 2:00 p.m.

At what time do you leave school?

I think it is nice to speak two languages in your house.

In my house we only speak Spanish, but I know how to speak English well.

I have one brother. His name is Mark and he is 13 years old. My sister Catalina is 5 years old.

I like to play tennis, basketball, volleyball, swimming and hockey in the grass.

What sports do you like to play?

I also play the organ and they are teaching me how to play the guitar.

What are your favorite colors?

(sic)   (sic)

Do you hear music? I hear music of rock and sometimes opera music.

Can you send me a picture of you?

Please write soon to this address. The address that you sent the card to is correct, but I want to receive your letter in my house.

(sic)

Sincerely,

Luisa

Querida Maria,

Estaba muy bonita la estampa que pusiste en mi carta.

Yo pienso que ha de ser bonito seleccionar estampas yo colecciono estamps y timbres postales.

A mi me gusta escuela solamente los viernes porque no tenemos tarea algunas veces alimos de la escuela a las 12:00 p.m. y normalmente salimos a las 2:00 p.m.

¿A que hora sales del a escuela?

Yo pienso que ha de ser bonito hablar dos idiomas en tu casa.

En mi casa solo hablamos español pero yo se hablar el inglés bien.

Tengo un hermano su nombre es David y tiene 12 anos. Mi hermana Catalina tiene 5 anos.

A mi me gusta jugar tenis básquetbol, volibol y, hockey sobre herboso.

¿Que deportes te gusta practicar?

Yo toco el organo y me estan ensanado a tocar la guitarra.

¿Te gusta oir música? Yo oigo música de rock y rara vez música de opera?

¿Me podrias mander una foto tuya?

Por favor escribe pronto a esta dirección la dirección donde mandaste la carta esta bien yo la quiero recibir en mi casa.

Sinceremente,

Luisa

Writing Reports

Naturally, your child has been busy writing paragraphs, stories and letters at school and home. However, perhaps he is a little frustrated because he has difficulty organizing his thoughts or doesn't know how to begin. It is not uncommon for children to feel anxious when writing the first paragraph of a report, letter or story, but there are a few tips which will help your child learn to love writing.

First, he must ask himself what he wants to write about. You may wish to review Chapter 3, page 61 to learn about selecting a topic. Once he has chosen a topic, he must limit the topic. For example, if he plans to write a short report on California, he may consider selecting a city in California to write about. He couldn't possibly cover all aspects of California in one short report; however, he can highlight some of the interesting features of a city in California.

Writing about Rocks and Minerals

Look at the partial report shown on page 126. The first sentence of this report is the topic sentence. Notice that the other two sentences in this first paragraph support the idea of the topic sentence. What are the changes?

ENVIRONMENTAL AND CHEMICAL.

124

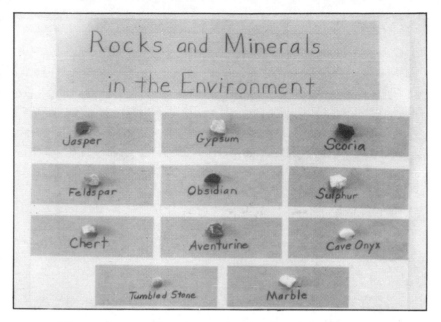

Now the reader is curious about how the environment and chemical reactions can actually change the earth's surface, so the writer must provide this information for him. This writer explains in further detail what is meant by environmental and chemical reactions so the reader has a clearer picture of how the environment and chemical reactions create changes in minerals and rocks.

The writer introduces two new terms, erosion and weathering. He then defines what weathering and erosion accomplish. The reader is then given an example of environmental factors that cause erosion.

The writer further defines the term weathering. The reader learns that there are two types of weathering, *physical* and *chemical*, Also, examples are given of each type so the reader can understand the different mechanisms involved.

125

Partial Report
Rocks and Minerals in Our Environment

The earth's surface is always changing. Many things are involved in causing this change. Some of the changes are caused by the environment while others are just the result of chemical reactions.

Our land is shaped by erosion and weathering. Weathering is a chemical and physical breakdown of rocks and minerals. From this breakdown new products are formed. Erosion is caused by things like the wind, glaciers and waves.

Weathering comes in two types, physical and chemical. During physical weathering the rocks are mechanically broken down into smaller pieces. In chemical weathering the minerals in the rock react to things like water, acids and oxygen.

In addition to writing the report, your child may enjoy making a poster like the one pictured on page 125. **The Rock & Gem Shop** in Anaheim, California is an excellent place to shop for supplies for this project. (**The Rock & Gem Shop, American Indian Store and The Stamps & Coins Shop** are all located in HOBBY CITY, Anaheim, California, so you can do all of the shopping for many of the projects listed in this book during one visit!)

Your child may be able to find some of the rocks and minerals on his own. However, for the poster project you may find it worth your while to purchase the *Rocks/Minerals Collection of 16.* You will find a nice selection of the following: granite, feldspar, calcite, agate, cave onyx, obsidian, sulphur, gypsum, amethyst, marble, scoria, chert, aventurine, quartz, jasper, and tumbled stone. This collection sells for about $3.00. **The Rock & Gem Shop** may be out of this selection so you may want to inquire about some of their other collections. The *Colorful Rocks and Minerals for the Student and Beginner* consists of 20 specimens; however, the rocks and minerals are much smaller in size. This collection sells for about $2.00. Finally, the *Gemstones of the World Collection* contains a beautiful array of gemstones from places like South Dakota, Brazil, South Africa, India, Zimbabwe, Mexico, etc. I purchased this collection at **The Rock & Gem Shop** two years ago, and, at that time it sold for $3.50. **The Rock & Gem Shop** has a beautiful array of rocks, minerals and gemstones. The personnel are friendly and knowledgable. Your child would undoubtedly learn a lot by listening to their conversations with customers. Moreover, your child would probably see more than one book or magazine here which would be of interest to him. Therefore, if you are in the Anaheim area, be sure to stop by on your way to Knott's Berry Farm or Disneyland. If you wish to write for ordering information, see page 146.

Combining Composition Skills with Health Education

Maria Montessori was very concerned about the health of children. As a physician she recognized the importance of diet in the overall health of a child. Meals prepared at the typical Montessori school are always nutritious, and the children are often encouraged to assist with preparing the food. Thus, the children learn in a natural, relaxed environment the importance of selecting and preparing wholesome foods.

You may encourage your child to do a little research on his own to determine the benefits of eating nutritious foods. He may wish to learn about combining foods using the Basic Four Food Groups. Then, suggest that he make menus for a day, week or perhaps for an entire month. Here is an example of a typical menu.

BREAKFAST
1 bowl of oatmeal
with milk and a little honey
1 glass or Orange Juice
1/2 banana

LUNCH
Peanut butter & jelly
sandwich on whole wheat
bread
1 glass of milk
1 orange

DINNER
Spaghetti with meatballs
1/4 cup of corn
1/4 cup of peas
1 small mixed green salad
with French dressing
1 glass of milk

SNACK
1 small box of raisins

SNACK
1 small glass of grape juice and
2 graham crackers

SNACK
Strawberry milkshake
(Made with fresh strawberries,
milk, honey and vanilla)

Your child may also enjoy making a chart showing which foods are high in particular nutrients. Encourage your child to select only three nutrients at a time, i.e. protein, vitamin A and calcium.

FOODS RICH IN
CALCIUM, PROTEIN AND VITAMIN A

FOODS RICH
IN CALCIUM

Milk
Cheese
Ice Cream
Baked Beans

FOODS RICH
IN VITAMIN A

Broccoli
Carrots
Kale
Pumpkins
Squash
Sweet Potato
Tomato
Apricots

FOODS RICH
IN PROTEIN

Baked Beans
Milk
Puddings
Ice Cream
Cheese
Yogurt
Beef
Eggs
Fish
Ham

Next, encourage your child to select a group of nutrients to write about. He may choose to write about lipids, proteins and carbohydrates or about minerals or vitamins.

Encourage your child to do adequate research at the library. He should have a pencil and some index cards handy so that he can jot down notes about what he learns during his research. Hopefully, he will borrow a few books on the subject to take home so that he can really discuss his topic in-depth. For example, if he is writing a report about the function of minerals in the human diet, he would first need to define what the minerals are, state the function of each mineral and list the foods which contain these minerals.

Next, he would write a rough draft. He now has the opportunity to organize his thoughts on paper and determine whether or not he knows enough about the subject to actually write his final draft. He may discover, at this point, that he needs to do additional research to verify his facts. Or, he may have an insufficient amount of data in which to substantiate his main idea.

The composition on page 131 opens with an introductory paragraph that presents the main idea. The introduction is then followed by five body paragraphs that develop the main idea. The last paragraph presents the conclusion of the report, reminding the reader of the ideas presented in the first paragraph.

EXAMPLE OF A REPORT
DONE BY A TYPICAL THIRD GRADER

VITAMINS AND YOUR HEALTH

Vitamins are very important for good health. Since our bodies require all of the vitamins to work properly we need to eat a variety of foods. One easy way to make sure that our bodies get a balanced supply of vitamins is to choose foods from each of the Basic Four Food Group.

Most of the vitamin B complex are found in whole wheat products like whole wheat bread, whole wheat muffins, whole wheat pancakes and in a variety of other foods. Since vitamin B is not just one vitamin, it is important to include all of the complex in our diet. Each vitamin has separate a function, but all of the B vitamins need to be present to work effectively.

Vitamin B1, thiamine, is in pork, legumes and whole grain products. Vitamin B2, riboflavin is found in cheese, veal, beef, broccoli, spinach, enriched cereal products and whole grain products to name a few. A good source for Vitamin B6, pyridoxine, includes the whole wheat products, whole grain cereals, vegetables and liver. B12, cyanocobalmin, is found in vegetables, fruits, legumes and cereals. Biotin, is found in liver, chicken, milk products, fruits and vegetables. A good source of folacin is liver, legumes and lettuce. Pantothenic Acid and Choline are also found in whole grain products, liver and fresh vegetables to name a few.

A daily glass of orange juice provides us with a good supply of vitamin C. Many fruits and vegetables are rich in this vitamin; therefore, we need to select foods from the Vegetable-Fruit group like lemons, tomatoes, strawberries, grapefruits, cantaloupes, potatoes, spinach, kale, and broccoli.

The Vegetable-Fruit group also gives us foods rich in vitamin A. If we eat broccoli, kale and spinach we receive vitamins A & C. Other foods like carrots, chard, pumpkin and

131

winter squash are also good sources of vitamin A which need to be included in our diet.

Fortified milk products from the Milk group give us some of the vitamin D that we need. Cod liver oil is also a good source of this vitamin, but many people will not take it. We also get this vitamin from exposing our skin to the sunlight.

The last two vitamins, vitamins E and K are usually not mentioned as much, but we must not forget their importance. Vitamin E is found in cereals and green vegetables. Vitamin K is made in the small intestine and colon in the body, but we also eat a variety of foods that have a small amount of this vitamin. Some of these foods include cheese, beef liver, whole wheat foods, broccoli, cabbage, lettuce and turnip greens.

Selecting foods from each of the four food groups every day takes some thought at first. After awhile, though, it becomes a habit. It's a good habit to form for life, because by eating properly we help ourselves to better health.

Fun Filled Grammar Exercises

If your child is still experiencing difficulty with sentence structure, encourage him to diagram sentences. Diagraming helps your child eliminate sentence fragments and incorrect subject-verb agreement. Many of my students enjoy diagraming sentences on a small chalkboard. Others enjoy using a magic slate; so you may want to consider purchasing one of these learning aids.

Introduce only two different types of sentences during a learning session so that your child doesn't feel pressured. Then, invite him to compose and diagram his own sentences on the chalkboard.

EXAMPLE:

S = Subject
V = Verb   Label the appropriate parts of speech in the sentence.

Next, invite your child to repeat this exercise using a different subject and verb.

EXAMPLE:

Children	learn
S	V

S = Subject
V = Verb

Once you feel that your child has mastered diagraming the simple sentence move on to presenting the imperative sentence. As you know, in the imperative sentence the subject is not directly stated but is understood to be "you".

EXAMPLE:
Stop!

You	stop
S	V

S = Subject
V = Verb

Much time should be spent on diagraming the simple sentence and then on the imperative sentence. Diagraming becomes an enjoyable learning exercise for the young student because it is done in a relaxed environment. Many of my students are delighted when they see me bring out the chalkboard because they know that diagraming will be presented during the learning session.

Here are additional diagraming exercises that your child will enjoy.

COMPOUND SUBJECTS WITH VERBS

EXAMPLE:
Mark and Maria have moved.

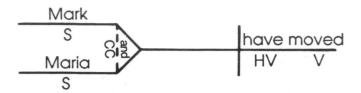

S = Mark (Subject)
S = Maria (Subject)
CC = and (Coordinating Conjunction)
HV = have (Helping Verb)
V = moved (Verb)

SUBJECT AND COMPOUND VERB

EXAMPLE:
Julio skipped and ran.

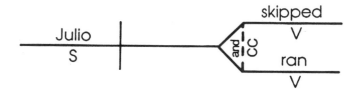

S = Julio (Subject)
V = skipped (Verb)
V = ran (Verb)
CC = and (Coordinating Conjunction)

135

SENTENCE CONTAINING PREDICATE ADJECTIVES

EXAMPLE:
The children were tired and hungry.

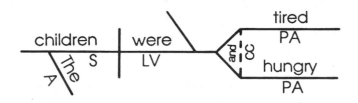

A = The (Article)
S = children (Subject)
LV = were (Linking Verb)
CC = and (Coordinating Conjunction)
PA = tired (Predicate Adjective)
PA = hungry (Predicate adjective)

Predicate adjectives typically are preceded by linking verbs, like *be, been, is, being, was* and *were*.

SENTENCES CONTAINING
PREDICATE NOUNS

EXAMPLE:
The tired swimmers are Julio and Peter.

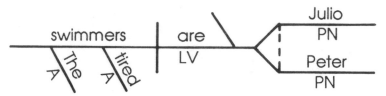

A = The (Article)
A = tired (Adjective)
S = swimmers (Subject)
LV = are (Linking Verb)
PN = Julio (Predicate Noun)
PN = Peter (Predicate Noun)

    Predicate nouns are also preceded by linking verb. Notice that in the preceding sentence "are" links the subject to the predicate.

SENTENCE CONTAINING AN ADVERB

EXAMPLE:
The playful puppy is very happy.

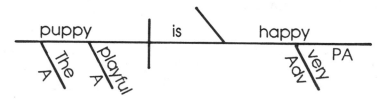

A = The (Article)
A = playful (Adjective)
S = puppy (Subject)
LV = LV is (Linking Verb)
ADV = very (Adverb)
PA = happy (Predicate Adjective)

SENTENCE CONTAINING
THE PREPOSITIONAL PHRASE

EXAMPLE:
The cat ran under the table.

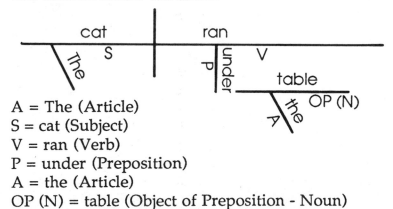

A = The (Article)
S = cat (Subject)
V = ran (Verb)
P = under (Preposition)
A = the (Article)
OP (N) = table (Object of Preposition - Noun)

Gaining General Knowledge Through Reading

Montessori wanted the child to satisfy his innate need for knowledge by participating in a learning environment which promotes self discoveries. In such an environment, the child would be given the tools in which to make these discoveries. Moreover, through these discoveries she felt the child would learn more about the world and his place in it.

One of the best tools that you can give your child is the **Young Discovery Library**. A total of 120 titles, many of which will be published by the time this book is in print, will give your child the information he needs to learn more about people, places, animals, natural resources, and the arts. The books are beautifully illustrated, complete with colorful drawings, diagrams, and in some cases, maps.

From **Oil to Plastics** is uniquely specific, explaining in a delightful way the conversion of oil to plastic. **Living in Ancient Rome** leads the young reader on an odyssey of Roman life circa the time of Christ. Beautifully detailed pictures accompanying the well written text leave the reader with the feeling that he has vicariously experienced life in that era.

I highly recommend that you purchase the complete set; however, I have listed each title for your ordering convenience. The books may be ordered through many bookstores. For additional information dial (800) 343-7854 or write **Young Discovery Library,** 217 Main Street, Ossining, New York 10562.

YOUNG DISCOVERY LIBRARY TITLES

Crocodiles and Alligators
Undersea Giants
Animals Underground
Elephants: Big, Strong & Wise
Animals in Winter
Long Ago in a Castle
On the Banks of Pharaoh's Nile
Living in Ancient Rome
Following Indian Trails
The Barbarians
Japan: Land of Samurai
Living with the Eskimos
Living on a Tropic Isle
Living in India
Australia: Other World
The Story of Paper
From Oil to Plastic
All About Wool
Metals: Earth and Fire
Grains of Salt
Going West: Cowboys and Pioneers
Blue Planet: Seas & Oceans
Bears, Big and Little
Cathedrals: Stone Upon Stone
Music! (Instruments - Orchestras)
Monkeys, Apes & Other Primates

Value Communications, Inc., located in San Diego, California, has developed a series called "The Value of Fantasy". These books are cleverly written and the illustrations are sure to delight the second or third grader as well as educate him about famous people like Hans Christian Andersen, Louis Pasteur, Helen Keller, Jackie Robinson and Benjamin Franklin, to name a few. I especially recommend the following titles:

The Value of Believing in Yourself:
    The Story of Louis Pasteur
The Value of Determination:
    The Story of Helen Keller
The Value of Patience:
    The Story of Wright Brothers
The Value of Humor:
    The Story of Will Rogers
The Value of Truth and Trust:
    The Story of Cochise
The Value of Caring:
    The Story of Eleanor Roosevelt
The Value of Curiosity:
    The Story of Christopher Columbus
The Value of Respect:
    The Story of Abraham Lincoln
The Value of Saving:
    The Story of Benjamin Franklin
The Value of Giving:
    The Story of Ludwig von Beethoven
The Value of Foresight:
    The Story of Thomas Jefferson
The Value of Fantasy:
    The Story of Hans Christian Anderson
The Value of Courage:
    The Story of Jackie Robinson

Finally, you may want to consider writing to **A Beka Books** for their latest catalog of educational items. **A Beka Books** publications is connected with Pensacola Christian College, and they publish a fine collection of books. These reading and social science books will help your child examine his own basic values, develop a sensitivity to the needs of others, and relate what he learns from reading these books to his own life. I highly recommend all of their books, i.e. math, reading, spelling, science, social science, etc: however, I will only list the reading books for grades one through four for your ordering convenience. You will find the address for **A Beka Books** on page 145.

First Grade:
Tiptoes
Stepping Stone
The Bridge Book
Open Windows
Merry-Go-Round
Aesop's Fables
Primary Bible Reader
Seesaw
Kind and Brave
Strong and True

Third Grade:
Footprints
Treat Shop
Crossroads
Paths to Follow
Secret in the Maple Tree
Better Bridges
Magic Carpet
Pilgrim's Progress Simplified

Second Grade:
Open Doors
Happiness Hill
Hidden Treasure
Open Roads
Primary Bible Reader
Paths of Gold
Pilgrim Boy
Silver Sails
Growing Up Where Jesus
    Lived
All Kinds of Animals
Tiptoes
Stepping Stones
Open Windows
Aesop's Fables

Fourth Grade:
Frontiers to Explore
Liberty Tree
Flags Unfurled
Enchanted Isles

142

Maria Montessori's mission for the child has been appreciated by educators, teachers and parents from every corner of the world. She used her innate gift of creativity and wisdom to devise lessons which would stimulate the child's interest in the world around him. She was wise enough to know that there had to be a better way for society to reach out to its children.

The child as a 'teacher' takes from the prepared environment what he needs to make the discoveries and spontaneous explosions involved with learning. However, we as educators, teachers and parents can assist the child by serving as his 'guide'. By presenting the child with the tools he needs to fulfill his potential, we accomplish two goals. First, the child climbs the ladder to becoming a self-actualized human being. Finally, as a society, we see the emergence of a caring, intelligent human being who will make a positive impact upon the environment. This was Maria Montessori's hope, and it should be our hope as well.

BIBLIOGRAPHY

Gebhardt-Steele, Peter G., The Computer and the Child: A Montessori Approach. Rockville, Maryland, Computer Science Press, Inc., 1985.

Montessori, Maria, The Absorbant Mind. New York, New York, The Dell Publishing Company, Inc. 1967.

Montessori, Maria, The Discovery of the Child. New York, New York, Ballatine Books, 1986.

Montessori, Maria, Education and Peace. Chicago, Illinois, Henry Regnery Company, 1972.

Montessori, Maria, Dr. Montessori's Own Handbook. New Yok, New York, Schoker Books, 1965.

Montessori, Maria, The Montesssori Method. Cambridge, Massachusetts, Robert Bentley, Inc. 1965.

Montessori, Maria, The Secret of Childhood. New York, New York, Ballatine Books, 1986.

Montessori, Maria, Spontaneous Activity in Education. Cambridge, Massachusetts, Robert Bentley, Inc. 1965.

APPENDIX A

Publishers of Recommended Books:

A BEKA BOOKS
118 St. John Street
Pensacola, FL 32523-9160

ESP, INC.
Publishers of Super Workbooks
1201 E. Johnson Avenue
Jonesboro, AR 72403-5080

LADYBIRD BOOKS, INC.
49 Omni Circle
P.O. Box 1690
Auburn, ME 04210

LAKESHORE CURRICULUM MATERIALS CO.
2695 E. Dominguez Street
Carson, CA 90749

PENDULUM PRESS, INC.
237 Saw Mill Road
West Haven, CT 06516

PLAYMORE, INC.
300 5th Avenue
New York, NY 10010

VALUE COMMUNICATIONS
3870 Murphy Canyon Road, Suite #203
San Deigo, CA 92123

APPENDIX B

Educational Resources for Lesson Planning

EARLY WORK LEARNING TOYS
P.O. Box 1657
San Anselmo, CA 94960

HOBBY CITY

American Indian Store	(714) 828-3050
Rock & Gem Shop	(714) 827-5680
Stamps & Coins	(714) 527-5866

1238 S. Beach Blvd.
Anaheim, CA 92804

IN-PRINT FOR CHILDREN
2113 Kenmore Avenue
Glenside, PA 19038

KINDERLINGS, INC,
978 Highlands Circle
Los Altos, CA 94022

LAKESHORE CURRICULUM
MATERIALS COMPANY
2695 E. Dominguez Street
Carson, CA 90749

THE MATERIALS COMPANY OF BOSTON
P.O. Box 608
Boston, MA 02102

APPENDIX B CONTINUED

RAINBOW MATERIALS CO., INC.
P.O. Box 2324
Woodinville, WA 98072

STUDENT LETTER EXCHANGE
630 3rd Avenue
New York, NY 10017

YOUNG DISCOVERY LIBRARY
217 Main Street
Ossining, NY 10562
(800) 343-7854

APPENDIX C

Selected Books for Lesson Planning

Arbuthnot, M.H. and Sutherland, Z. 1972. <u>Children and Books</u>. Scott, Foresman and Company, Glenview

Bender, Lionel, 1988. <u>Plants</u>. Glucester Press, New York.

Bingham, J.M. 1988. <u>Writers for Children</u>. Charles Scribner's Sons, New York.

Broekel, R. 1988. <u>Experiments With Water.</u> Childrens Press, Chicago.

Brown, B. and Brown, W. 1970. <u>Historical Catastrophes: Volcanoes</u>. Adison-Wesley Publishing Co., Inc., Reading

Brown, R.J., 1987. <u>200 Illustrated Science Experiments for Children.</u> Tab Books, Inc, Blue Ridge Summit

Crowson, P. 1982. <u>Minerals Handbook.</u> Van Nostrand Reinhold, New York.

Curzio, C. and Borelli, A. 1986. <u>Simon & Schuster's Gem and Precious Stones.</u> Simon & Schuster, New York.

Desautels, P.E. 1974. <u>Collector's Series: Rocks & Minerals,</u> Grosset & Dunlap Publishers, New York.

Douvaiens, F., Beatrice, T. and Marchand, P. 1971. <u>Seaside Treasures</u>. Random House of Canada Limited, Toronto.

Ford, R. and Strimpel, O. 1985. <u>Computers: An Introduction</u>. Orbis Publishing Limited, London.

Gay, K. 1988. Science in Ancient Greece. Franklin Watts, New York.

Gray, M. and Deutch, Y. 1975. Rainy Day Pastimes: 215 Ideas To Keep Children Happy. Publications Limited, London.

Hutchings, M. 1972. Making New Testament Toys. Taplinger Publishing Company, New York.

Lickteig, M.J. 1975. An Introduction to Children's Literature. Charles E. Merrill Publishing Co., Columbus.

McKibbin, J. and McKibbin, F. 1972. Cookbook of Foods from Bible Days. Voice Publications, Culver City.

Mitchell, R.S., 1985. Dictionary of Rocks. Van Nostrand Reinhold, New York.

Mitchell, R.S., 1979. Mineral Names: What Do They Mean? Van Nostrand Reinhold Company, New York.

Rosenberg, J.K., 1977. Young People's Literature in Series. Libraries Unlimited, Inc. Littleton.

Schumann, W. 1984. Gemstones of the World. Sterling Publishing, Inc., New York.

Sorrell, C.A. 1973. A Guide to Field Identification of Rocks & Minerals. Golden Press, New York.

Went, F., 1980. Life Nature Library: The Plants. Time-Life Books, Morristown.

Woods, G. 1988. Science in Ancient Egypt. Franklin Watts, New York.

149

APPENDIX D

Selected Health and Science Books for Children

Blough, G.O., 1966. Disovering Plants. McGraw-Hill Book Company, New York. (Second Grade Level)

Gaskin, J. 1985. The Heart. Franklin Watts, New York. (Second Grade Level)

Ward, R.B., 1982 The Heart and Blood. Franklin Watts, New York. (Third Grade Level)

Weisgard, L. 1956. Treasures to See: A Museum Picture-Book. Harcourt, Brace Jovanovich, New York. (Second Grade Level)

White, A.T. and Lietz, G.S. 1965. Secrets of the Heart and Blood. Garrard Publishing Co., champaign (Fourth Grade Level)

Wong, O.K. 1986. Your Body and How It Works. Childrens Press, Chicago. (Fourth Grade Level)

APPENDIX E

Selected Social Science Books for Children Six through Nine years of Age

Bains, R. 1985. Indians of the Eastern Woodlands. Troll Associates, Mahway (Second Grade Level)

Bernheim, E. 1969. A Week in Aya's World: The Ivory Coast. Crowell-Collier Press, London (Third Grade Level)

Crosher, J. 1976. The Aztecs. Silver Burdett Company, Morristown. (Second Grade Level)

Glubok, S. 1975. The Art of the Plains. MacMilliam Publishing, Co., Inc. New York. (First Grade Level)

Hargreaves, P. 1981. The Arctic. Silver Burdett, Morristown (Fourth Grade Level)

Hargreaves, P. 1981. The Caribbean & Gulf of Mexico. Silver Burdett, Morrisstown. (Fourth Grade Level)

Hinds, L. 1973. Looking at Great Britain. J.B. Lippincott Company, Philadelphia. (Third Grade Level)

McGovern, A. 1975. The Secret Soldier.. Four Winds Press, New York. (Third Grade Level)

Meshover, L. 1967. You Visit A Museum Library. Benefic Press, Chicago.

Phelan, M.K. 1966. The Fourth of July. Tom Y. Crowell Company, New York. (Second Grade Level)

Walton, D. 1985. What Color Are You? An Ebony Jr. Book, Johnson Publishing Company, Inc., Chicago (Second Grade Level)

APPENDIX F

Dictionaries and Reference Books for Children Six through Nine years of Age

Cooney, B. 1960. <u>The American Speller.</u> Thomas Y. Crowell Company, New York. (Third Grade Level)

Halsey, W.D., 1987. <u>MacMillian Dictionary for Children.</u> MacMillan & Company, New York. (Second Grade Level)

Haywood, L. 1980. <u>The Sesame Street Dictionary</u>. Random House, New York. (First Grade Level)

Kohn, B. 1976. <u>Whatchamacallit Book.</u> G.P. Putnam's Sons, New York. (Second Grade Level)

Lipton, G. and Munoz, O. 1975. <u>Spanish Bilingual Dictionary.</u> Barron's Educational Series, Inc., Hauppauge (Fourth Grade Level)

Terban, M. 1984. <u>I Think I Thought and Other Tricky Verbs</u>. Clarion Books, New York. (Second Grade Level)

Terban, M. 1986. <u>Your Foot's On My Feet & Other Tricky Nouns.</u> Clarion Books, New York. (Second Grade Level)

APPENDIX G

Selected Religious Books for Children

McElderry, M.K. 1983. <u>Jonah and The Great Fish</u>. Athenum, New York. (Second Grade Level)

Petersham, M. 1958. <u>Joseph and His Brothers</u>. The MacMillian Company, New York. (First Grade Level)

Simon, N. 1965. <u>Passover</u>. Thomas T. Crowell Company, New York. (First Grade Level)

APPENDIX H

Additional Reading Books for Children

Hadithi, M. 1987 <u>Crafty Chameleon</u>. Little, Brown and
    Company, Boston. (First Grade Level)

Lasked, D. 1979. <u>The Boy Who Loved Music.</u> The Viking Press,
    New York. (Second Grade Level)

Montgomery, J. 1959. <u>Foxy</u>. Franklin Watts, Inc., New York.
    (Fourth Grade Level)

Montgomery, J. 1961. <u>My Friend Foxy</u>. Franklin Watts, Inc.
    New York. (Fourth Grade Level)

Politi, L. 1979. <u>Song of the Swallows</u>. Charles Scribner's Sons,
    New York. (Second Grade Level)

Scott, J. and Scott, L. 1983. <u>Hieroglyphs for Fun: Your Own
    Secret Code Language.</u> Van Nostrand Reinhold
    Company, New York. (Thrid Grade Level)

INDEX

155